PARIS
IN BLOOM

TEXT BY

DENISE LE DANTEC

JEAN-PIERRE LE DANTEC

PHOTOGRAPHS BY

CHRISTOPHER BAKER

FLAMMARION

EDITORIAL DIRECTION
BY GHISLAINE BAVOILLOT

EDITING BY LISA DAVIDSON

DESIGN BY MARC WALTER

TYPESETTING BY OCTAVO EDITIONS

CAPTIONS, GARDEN GUIDE AND
FLORAL CALENDAR BY CLAUDINE DURAND

MAP BY LÉONIE SCHLOSSER

TRANSLATED FROM THE FRENCH BY BAMBI BALLARD

THE TRANSLATION OF THIS VOLUME WAS ASSISTED BY A GRANT FROM
THE FRENCH MINISTRY OF CULTURE AND COMMUNICATION.

SIMULTANEOUSLY PUBLISHED IN FRANCE UNDER THE TITLE
SPLENDEURS DES JARDINS DE PARIS
PRINTED AND BOUND BY ARTI GRAFICHE MOTTA, MILAN

FLAMMARION
26, RUE RACINE
75006 PARIS

CONTENTS

FOREWORD

Just as the paintings of Canaletto first revealed Venice, the camera lens of Alfred Stieglitz captured New York, and the novels of Charles Dickens evoked London, it was the Impressionists who first introduced us to Paris. And at the heart of their profoundly analytical response to the new Paris of the Second Empire — with its boulevards, public spaces, railroad stations and rural environs used by Parisians seeking to escape the city — there were always gardens.

Whether we gaze down upon the tree-lined boulevard Haussmann with Gustave Caillebotte; examine with Édouard Manet the raw, new escarpment of the Trocadéro; follow Berthe Morisot through the Bois de Boulogne to watch the bourgeoisie at leisure; dance under the trees in the Tuileries with Manet's crowds; watch over the Jardin d'Enfants with Claude Monet; escape to the overgrown garden of Pierre-Auguste Renoir's studio on the rue Cortot; or stumble upon the small vernacular gardens in Montmartre that entranced Armand Guillaumin — all these finely nuanced images of gardens are an ineluctable part of Impressionist Paris.

Regardless of what brings us to Paris, no matter what our purpose, business or pleasure, we cannot ignore its open and verdant spaces.

They date from many different periods: for more than four centuries they were created throughout Paris in a way that is unique among large cities. And the abundance of them! The Bois de Boulogne and the Bois de Vincennes enclose the city in huge green parentheses. Parks punctuate the different *quartiers*, and each expresses a special sense of place. The grid of boulevards that follows the tree-lined city walls fans out into avenues of trees, especially along the Champs-Élysées (named after the ultimate garden in Greek mythology). There are many private gardens that can be glimpsed through archways, while remaining tantalizingly out of reach beyond the formidable barrier of concierges. And there are the much more accessible but somber cemeteries, which offer what nineteenth-century Americans were told was provided by Laurel Hill in Philadelphia, a "book of nature and human destiny, which is ever read with interest and profit."

Then there are the Tuileries, the austere Palais-Royal, the Luxembourg Gardens, the Jardin des Plantes (apparently — though on reflection it is not surprising — the fourth most popular tourist attraction in the city). Last but by no means least are the "squares", created by Napoleon III because he so loved those in London, yet — as the noted English garden writer William Robinson was quick to remark in 1869 — those in Paris are much more democratic than their British counterparts.

It is into this inexhaustible variety of Parisian gardens that Denise Le Dantec and Jean-Pierre Le Dantec lead us, in a book that will suit the armchair traveler and gardener as well as the stroller or *flâneur* along Parisian streets. Between them, brother and sister, the authors are poet, philosopher and architectural historian, and have already brought this triad of perspectives to bear upon the history of French gardens in an imaginative and provoking study, *Reading the French Garden* (MIT Press, 1990). Their new book is clearly written with the same poetic insight and turn of phrase, with attention paid to the metaphysical as well as to the physical dimension of the garden, and with a keen historical appetite for all the strata of the garden palimpsest encountered on so many Parisian sites.

We need much more urban garden history. Attention is more usually and more lovingly devoted to country seats than to city gardens; yet if gardens are the supreme art of *milieu*,

we should seek the most eloquent expressions of human response to both space and nature in the more confined and endlessly threatened arenas of city dwelling. Parisians have become particularly alert to the urban history of their city, and several exhibitions in the early 1980s (concerning the Parc Monceau, for example, and the various streets and *quartiers*) have drawn upon rich archives to explore this emerging garden history.

This appealing volume responds to and continues that *politique culturelle* with a wide range of references and with its own enthusiasms for planting and design, trees and trelliswork, for the stylistic oppositions between the seventeenth and nineteenth centuries, for tensions between public and private, for social and topographical differences, for that huge delight in gardens as theaters for that combination of learning and absurdity, pleasure and thoughtfulness that the Parisian exemplifies par excellence.

JOHN DIXON HUNT
Academic Advisor to the Oak
Spring Garden Library

INTRODUCTION

What could be more universal than the art of gardening? From the beginning of time it has given form to humanity's most persistent dream: that of creating a perfect harmony between man and nature. Doubtless this is a chimera kept alive by nostalgia for a lost paradise and the hopes of a golden age. According to Roberto Burle Marx, one of the most important landscapists of the twentieth century, the garden is an attempt to represent "the fundamental contact between man and nature as the perfect link between the small interior world and the immense exterior world, in order to reestablish a proper balance and to attain serenity." It can be modest or accomplished, simple or sophisticated, it may display a profusion of plants or an abundance of mineral elements: whatever its manifestation, the aim of a garden is to depict the mind confronted with the mystery of the world. As fields of consciousness, enigma and energy, man and nature are interlinked through unceasing transformation, so is a garden an endlessly renewed adventure.

Very few large cities have had the history and the climate to create such a great variety of gardening styles and such a varied panoply of plants as Paris. An ordered formality cohabits with the picturesque, and certain trees, once exotic, are so well acclimatized they are now commonplace. This extraordinary accomplishment is the result of an ancient culture in which nature was able to take form and flourish. It is therefore good news for garden lovers that Paris has recently reviewed its landscaping policies. The renovation of major historical gardens, which should return them to their original glory, and the creation of new gardens is underway, inspired by an admirable intellectual audacity.

When Henry Miller returned to New York after Nazi troops occupied the "capital of the twentieth century," he nostalgically described that unique Parisian gray that "brings a whole world of ideas and sensations to life" and whose range "seems without end."

The city of Verlaine and the Impressionist painters is a city of nuance, created by the delicate sky, the qualities of the Île-de-France stone and the morning light that is so subtle it almost seems to be a silver powder softly falling on the Seine. The mornings are therefore the best time for strolling with poet Jacques Réda through the "sweet thickening of the grayness" in quest of Paris's gardens, where even the most ordinary square offers an unexpected treasure and the flowering lawns brighten the pale sky.

1

JARDINS

A LA FRANÇAISE

Paris gardens, those civilized, graceful and beautiful reminders of the city's past, are at their best in the autumn, when the sky is suffused with dazzling pink rays and imbued with the sadness of the waning season.

The voluptuous statues in the Tuileries, decked in golden leaves from the tall chestnut trees, create an intoxicating contrast with the formal splendor of the gardens. The spectacle of the softly falling leaves never loses its enchantment. It is a contemplative scene, one that inspires reflections about the past and art, about grace and movement. Former cultures and civilizations seem to be even more present as the skies darken and the remaining, bare flower beds offer yet another side of nature, a melancholic one in the cool light of autumn.

Summer offers an entirely different vision: entering through the gate on the rue de Rivoli — and bypassing the romantic abandon of the English-style shrubbery — is like stepping into the exhilarating atmosphere of the *Grand Siècle*. The "moat" at this entrance that separated the defunct private gardens from the vast public area is still visible. Early spring reflects yet another facet of the magnificent garden; the colorful flower beds brighten the lawns of the Louvre, and even the Champs-Élysées as far as the Arc de Triomphe.

In winter this royal garden becomes a mere thoroughfare across which Parisians hasten briskly. Its pair of long icy terraces are then only — to quote Marcel Poëte — "a dead body lying on a history-filled piece of earth." The sculptures, including *The Tigers* and other

Beds of flowers wrapped inside small hedges of boxwood in the Tuileries evoke the memory of the prodigious French-style design bequeathed by Le Nôtre (above). A marble group by Van Cleve stands in front of the octagonal basin in the Tuileries; it came from Marly — which was destroyed — a castle once as splendid as Versailles (facing).

wild animals sculpted by Auguste Cain; the mythological groupings; and the allegories of the *Rivers* or *Seasons* sculpted by the official artists of the nineteenth century — all retain a handsome grandeur, especially when the pounding rain, clouding the view, glances off the bronze and marble backs of the statues with the crashing sound of hunting horns.

Because of the tragic destruction inflicted by man and fate — riots, devastation, fires, misuse and lack of maintenance — the Tuileries Gardens offer only a shadow of their former glory. Yet this does not diminish the pleasure of exploring the tree-lined alleys. Aside from enjoying the sheer beauty of the site, one keenly senses the history of Paris, and of France. It is a glorious history, and the bright

flame of the sparkling figures who shaped it shines there still, in the heart of Paris.

This is, indeed, the heart of the city. André Le Nôtre redesigned the Tuileries Gardens shortly after he landscaped the Luxembourg Gardens, thereby creating a series of marvels that is aptly named *à la française*.

Although the Luxembourg Gardens are very different from what they were in the Baroque period when Boyceau de la Bareaudière created them, they nevertheless reflect an aspect of the French character which is, first and foremost, Parisian.

The midday sun on a spring day illuminates a short avenue and creates a play of light that extends from the palace to the garden, highlighting the precise layout and the exquisite refinement of the site. In the center of this oft-remodeled landscape reigns an absolute stillness in which the garden's former order, beauty and glory seem to come alive: a corner of a pond becomes incandescent, memory is set alight, and sparks illuminate parties where royal pleasures were once indulged. Yet the image is a fleeting one and other, more recent, lights sweep the memories away. Despite the short vistas, the Luxembourg Gardens continue to impress us with a disturbing fusion of majestic proportions, bourgeois intimacy and student leisure.

Sunday afternoon visitors — drawn outside by a spell of good weather — still crowd around the puppet show, the bandstand and the ice-cream vendors, while a solitary stroller, seated by one of the eight tropical palm trees, muses over his novel. Later in the year, winter wraps the gardens in ice and snow, and the picturesque, statue-filled woods, deprived of their opulent foliage, are returned to their underlying sparseness.

"Little Nice," situated in the curve of the grand staircase near the octagonal basin in the Tuileries, is a welcoming spot where elderly people come to enjoy the sun (above). The carefully structured design and multicolored flower beds in the Luxembourg Gardens are a constant delight to the stroller (facing). Autumn envelops the Luxembourg Gardens in golden and copper colors, when the soft and dusky light is propitious for poetic reveries beneath the chestnut trees (following page).

The Chalgrin walkway that leads to the Orangery, dividing the garden from east to west, is bordered with plane trees, many of which were planted as long ago as 1840. Inside the Orangery, there is an amazing collection of orange, bitter-orange and bergamot trees, of pomegranate and palm trees. The pink oleanders, which are moved outside in late spring, are said to date from the days of Marie de' Medici, the founder of the gardens. This is where Olivier de Serres, "the father of French agriculture," brought the first of his orange trees as a gift to King Henry IV. The Huguenot squire — a peasant and warrior, but also the author of *Le Théâtre de l'agriculture* (Theater of Agriculture) and *Le Mesnage des champs* (Theater of the Fields) — managed to grow the trees on his lands at Pradel, in the Vivarais. Delighted, the king bought hundreds of orange trees and had them shipped to Paris.

The southern half of the Luxembourg Gardens, although "landscaped" in the nineteenth-century style, does not detract from the harmony of the whole. It merely encourages strollers to slow their pace and to examine at leisure the busts of former habitués such as Watteau (who drew his inspiration for the *Fêtes Galantes* landscapes from the gardens), the nineteenth-century poets Heredia, Baudelaire and Verlaine, writer Sainte-Beuve and composer Massenet. Clumps of colorful flowers brighten the lawns. A multitude of tits sing as they flutter from the flowering privets full of nectar to the great aucubas with huge, shiny, oval leaves. There used to be a path, along which the peasants led their flocks, running along what is now the rue Notre-Dame-des-Champs. Catherine de' Medici bought several mansions here, including the one belonging to Piney-Luxembourg, for whom the property is named. In 1615 Salomon de Brosse built a palace for her younger cousin, Marie de' Medici, a little

farther to the east, which was reminiscent of her childhood home, the Palazzo Pitti in Florence. She asked Jacques Boyceau de la Bareaudière to create a garden inspired by the Boboli gardens. The great artist and author of the first manifesto of the French style, *Le Traité de jardinage selon les raisons de l'art et de la nature* (Treatise of Gardening According to the Reasons of Art and Nature, 1638), improved upon the Italian model and enlarged it by expanding to the west. He was limited to the south by the Chartreux domain, which did not become part of the Luxembourg Gardens until the early nineteenth century. Boyceau chose a plan that was essentially Italian, transforming it into a work that was absolutely French, both in form and in spirit.

In winter, the empty chairs in the Luxembourg Gardens share their solitude with the pensive statues (above). Legendary figures can be seen in this garden, which is a paradise for children; thus, the owner of small carts for hire was the character Nounours in a French television cartoon in the 1960s (facing).

Although Boyceau's work was later adapted to suit nineteenth-century bourgeois tastes, the spirit of his great design survives. And these origins still offer a precious aura of peace in the midst of the religious, cultural and artistic center that later became Montparnasse, the Latin Quarter and Saint-Sulpice.

The Palais-Royal and its gardens were built in 1629, shortly after the Luxembourg Gardens. Once one of the centers of French history, it owes much of its charm to the fact that it was built according to the severely elegant style of the seventeenth and eighteenth centuries. It forms a square, enclosed on three sides by colonnades of shops with private apartments above them. The fourth side is occupied by the palace itself, which faces the rue Saint Honoré and Place du Palais-Royal.

Although the Palais-Royal is comparatively small with strict, subdued lines, it nevertheless offers the strange impression of a place without a heart, as if only those rows of parallel trees photographed obliquely by Cartier-Bresson in the 1960s have survived. It still looks now as it must have appeared to some of its most prestigious earlier residents, such as Cocteau, Malraux and Colette.

The lime trees inside the garden that run parallel to the rue de Valois rustle gently after a rain shower and their leafy shadows are reflected in the glistening asphalt. Did Colette, author, wanderer and music-hall star, open the windows of her magnificent apartment on those nights when, like so many elderly people, she suffered from insomnia? Did she then breathe in the historic scents of the famous

*Light playing off the dead leaves forms a delicate
Impressionist composition in the pool of the Medici fountain (above).
On this fountain at the end of a romantic waterway,
Polyphemus bends over a rock to surprise Actis and Galactea
in a tender embrace (facing).*

garden? Could she perhaps have smelled the vapors of the Roman *Campelli*, which divided the former gardens of Cardinal Mazarin's Palace (now the National Library)? She may have met the ambiguous specter of Richelieu, Marie de' Medici's almoner, wandering through the arcades. He bought property here in 1629, although the only remaining trace is the Galerie des Proues, decorated with anchors denoting the fact that he was also the queen's naval superintendent. Or perhaps Colette saw the ghosts of Anne of Austria and her two sons, one of whom became Louis XIV, for Richelieu left his palace to Louis XIII provided that he, in turn, leave it to his descendants. Or even that of Mazarin, who accompanied the Queen Regent on her walks and watched over the children's games.

In the seventeenth century this historic garden was huge, bordered by a wood and surrounded by an elm-lined walkway, adorned with flower beds, shrubbery, statues and two large ponds in which the future Sun King narrowly escaped drowning. A horse track and a miniature fort were added for Louis XIII's sons. For many years the garden was reserved for children's games; its vocation changed abruptly after Louis XIV gave it to Monsieur, his brother Philippe d'Orléans. During this period the Palais-Royal became a brilliant center for the arts and sciences; it was also a renowned pleasure site, well known for its "ladies of the night." A few years later, before he embraced the revolutionary cause and voted for his cousin Louis XVI's death, Louis-Philippe, the future Philippe Egalité, built a ring of arcades and commercial galleries that made the Palais-Royal look very similar to how it appears today. By creating a series of boutiques and apartments around the formerly open space, he enclosed the garden and reduced its proportions. Nevertheless, the intellectual, artistic and licentious pursuits that had flourished under Philippe d'Orléans were allowed to continue.

"Rain or shine," Diderot wrote in *Le Neveu de Rameau*, "I always go for a stroll around the Palais-Royal at five o'clock. I am always alone, sitting on Argenson's bench, dreaming. I talk to myself about politics, love, good taste or philosophy. I let my mind wander freely, and allow it to pursue the first wise or foolish thought that appears, like a dissolute youth following the steps of a wanton courtesan with a smiling face, bright eyes and a turned-up nose along the Foy gallery, only to leave her for another, approaching them all but taking none of them up. My thoughts are my whores. If it is too cold or too wet, I take shelter in the Régence café, and pass the time watching the games of chess."

In the second half of the eighteenth century, journalists, philosophers, gamblers, adventurers and prostitutes met at the Palais-Royal. The gardens were a haven of freedom, somewhat loose in moral tenor, but intellectual enough to draw praise from Sébastien Mercier, who claimed that "you will find nothing like it in London, Amsterdam or Madrid." The arcades were filled with flower shops and boutiques selling knickknacks, with glassed-in pavilions for drinking chocolate at midday or eating ice-cream at five o'clock. There were bands and traveling players, but, even though it was a place of pleasure, it was also a hotbed of revolutionary politics: "Citizens, we have not a moment to lose . . ." cried the handsome Camille Desmoulins, standing on a table on the summer afternoon of July 12, 1789. The call to arms against Charles X was also launched from the Palais-Royal on another July day in 1830, which resulted in the *Trois Glorieuses* and the capture of the Tuileries.

Between these two dates, the Palais-Royal reached the height of its popularity: the pursuit of pleasure and even the Stock Exchange picked up after the Terror. Under the romantic light of the gas lamps, along

The Palais-Royal lies isolated in the midst of the surrounding stone buildings. By dawn, various birds, including the black swift — which arrive from Africa in the spring — emerge from their alcoves (facing). The pilasters on the façades of the galleries in the Palais-Royal are decorated with acanthus leaves that turn into gracious volutes (following page). When the sun hits the tips of the trees, it is truly delightful to wander leisurely in the shade of the lime trees in the Palais-Royal (following page).

the flower beds, the officers of the Empire, and later, those commanding the troops that defeated Napoleon, danced with the prostitutes far into the night.

It is not surprising that Balzac set his *Comédie humaine* here, describing it as "a place that at nightfall becomes the haunt of every crook in Paris, the shame of society: crowds of gamblers, the leisured, the unemployed and the countless vagrants that people the city mingle there with girls of all kinds and even with apprentices." The Second Empire preferred the Tuileries Gardens, also a fashionable meeting point for high society and politics, but frequented by a "better" class of people.

From then on the Palais-Royal was somewhat forgotten, despite its central location between the Louvre, the Stock Exchange and the *Grands Boulevards*, and despite the presence of the famous restaurant Le Grand Véfour in one of the galleries. Even the highly publicized intervention of the sculptor Buren in 1985 did not revive it. The Goncourt brothers had already remarked that it was mainly frequented by "rich provincials and nostalgic Orléanists. In the cafés, the waiters were as discreet, respectful and silent as those hired to serve in the ministries." In fact, the garden today — closed in on three sides by galleries supported on fluted pilasters giving an effect of columns in perspective, and by the Palais-Royal itself on the fourth — is surprisingly quiet, considering that it lies in one of the busiest areas in Paris. Between midday and two o'clock a few solitary office workers come to eat their sandwiches before indulging in the luxury of a coffee on a terrace. Between five and six o'clock, a few couples stroll under the plane trees in the Place André Malraux, or in the Galerie d'Orléans, or beyond the first courtyard to the Cour d'Honneur, squared by Buren's truncated black and white columns, or to Pol Bury's two fountains, where the

polished steel spheres add a slow rolling movement to the jets of water. A single fan-shaped spray of water recalls the beautiful women of an earlier time. Everything is strangely calm in this place filled with rows of square-cut lime trees, the two chestnut trees, the flowering lawns and roses. What happened to the "excesses" of just over a century ago?

Although the gardens inside the wall of Paris, including the French-style Jardin des Plantes, retain something of a classical spirit, urbanization and the accompanying land and property speculation have shortened their vistas and diminished their size. Walking down rue Guynemer, along the noble railings of the Luxembourg Gardens, it is difficult to imagine the central axis as Boyceau first conceived it, extending as far as what is now the rue de Fleurus. It is equally hard to picture how the Tuileries Gardens must have looked in the days of Louis XIV; forests once stood on what is now the Champs-Élysées, and these opened out into the surrounding hunting grounds. Only outside of Paris does the breadth and nobility of these open spaces remain, and one of the most marvelous examples is the Parc de Sceaux.

Built on a fairly even terrain, this masterpiece, now stripped of its lawns, woods and statues,

One of the two chestnut trees in the Palais-Royal emerges
here along the axis of the large basin, where in summer a fan of water
sparkles in the sun (above and facing).

has become pure geometry since it was renovated in 1920 by Jean-Claude-Nicolas Forestier and Louis Azéma. Reduced to a series of mirrors studded with stones, framed by immense lawns that stand out against a background of lofty woods, it has been returned to its original nature. Once stripped of its adornments by history, the garden was able to conjure up, from its skeletal frame, its stern Jansenist structure.

The Parc de Sceaux was designed by Le Nôtre for Colbert, a rigid finance minister so jealous of Fouquet and his gardens at Vaux-le-Vicomte that he not only persuaded the young Louis XIV to requisition his superintendent's property, but also to imprison for life its brilliant owner. Thus Colbert, whose coat of arms was a snake (*coluber* means snake), got

his little Sceaux, while the king got his masterpiece, by ordering Le Nôtre, Le Vau and Le Brun — all one-time companions of Fouquet's — to create Versailles.

The park has two enormous walks. One is lined with lime trees and leads to the rebuilt palace, while the other, the allée de Diane, intersects the first and leads to the great waterfalls, coming to an end at a vast octagonal pond. This pond, and the wide canal that runs north to south into it, form a sheet of water from which rises a twenty-five-meter spray like a flame of glittering air. Great cascades fall from terraced basins to form a giant staircase of water slipping softly down to the fields that have replaced most of the woods, lawns and statues that once studded the walks. Stripped to its bare bones, Sceaux

These conical yews, pruned only twice a year, add a playful note to the almost too-perfect rigor of the Parc de Sceaux (above). Despite its classical form, the Grand Canal de Sceaux flows like a peaceful river, bordered by high Italian poplars (facing). The Hanover pavilion — previously in the gardens of the sumptuous residence of the Duc de Richelieu in Paris — stands at the end of the alleys, beyond the water-filled basins (following page).

beats a muffled drum, its contours traced by air, water and light. But it springs into life with the slightest change of light, especially at nightfall. Its boundaries then become blurred and one feels a great desire to linger there, a prisoner of the waning light as it pauses above the watery expanse. This stretch of water never ceases to amaze even if, as has been suggested, this thing of beauty was born of a torrent of tears shed by La Fontaine, in memory of his banished friend:

"Fill the air with your cries from your deep grottoes
Mourn [him], O Nymphs of Vaux . . ."

However, there is another park that, even more than Sceaux, performs the miracle of uniting water, stone and verdure in a breathtaking

harmony, for it is built on a nobler site, facing the Seine: the Parc de Saint-Cloud.
This masterpiece — also designed by Le Nôtre, but this time for *Monsieur*, Louis XIV's brother — was part of a vast domain. The palace, which was burned in the war of 1870, was built to the specifications of Mansart, and so superbly done that, in Corneille's opinion, it was "the most beautiful palace in all of France." The main axis of the park is oriented straight down the hill, contrary to the lateral terraces laid out along level lines that were popular during the Italian, French and Palatine Renaissance. A tremendous amount of clearing, filling in and banking, as well as hydraulics and draining, must have gone into a work that so absolutely defied nature. Around a perfectly regular axis, the grounds are terraced in short successive levels that

These statues in the Parc de Sceaux, which are among the most beautiful bronzes from the Louis XIV era, belong to a group called The Subjected Nations *(above). The tulips are the real sign of spring, at Sceaux as in all Parisian gardens (facing).*

widen into clumps of shrubbery and flowers, or that surround a pond. It is a prodigious work in which nature has been mastered, or rather, has been reinstated to its "real," fundamentally geometric, aspect.

In seventeenth-century France, geometry was the supreme science, invented — or reinvented — by Baroque thinkers such as Pascal, Desargues and La Hire, and by the more classical, analytical philosophers Descartes and Roberval, to serve as the golden measure of the physical and intellectual world. The scholars and philosophers of the day explained that nature was fundamentally geometric; it appears irregular only by accident. According to Boyceau — who worked with space and vegetation in accordance with the laws of nature and

art — the gardener's task was therefore to reveal the inherent geometry of a site by restraining it, and, through pruning and training, to reproduce the geometric forms that secretly inhabit plants. French gardens have often been accused of being "anti-natural," yet every author, beginning with Dézallier d'Argenville, states the opposite, and criticizes the "outrages" of the past in the name of that same "nature." But "natural" was not then associated with freedom, as it is today: for the masters of the *Grand Siècle*, "natural" meant following the divine rules of nature.

Beyond the Cour d'Honneur and the yew trees that mark the site of the palace in Saint-Cloud stretch the private gardens, which include a pond, the lawns of the Orangery

The pools, from which emerge an occasional huge jet of water, are one of the most attractive elements in the Parc de Saint-Cloud (above). Cathedrals of green and unexpected views contribute to the splendor of this park (facing). The majestic stairs at Saint-Cloud descend slowly toward Paris, enticing the stroller into a landscape of towns and mists (following page).

and the Rond-Point des Vingt-Quatre Fontaines. Above it, the Trocadéro, a garden now cultivated in the English style, overlooks the empty space where the palace one stood, while a waterfall and a jet of water grace the lower garden at the base of the terrace.

The large expanse of lawn, the fountains, the tall column of water and the Rond-Point des Balustrades — all designed by Le Nôtre and his pupils — contribute to the irresistible charm of the immense park of Saint-Cloud.

Virtually all the gardens of the Paris museums can be included with these gardens dedicated to culture and art: the flower beds at the Carnavalet Museum, where Madame de Sevigné found "fresh air, a beautiful courtyard, a beautiful garden"; the garden at the Rodin

Museum; and the neoclassical garden of the Renan-Scheffer Museum. All give an idea of the beauty of the private gardens that still lie behind the townhouses and villas of Paris, most of which are in the 16th arrondissement or in the Marais.

Between 1960 and 1970 — after the "clean-up operation" of the courtyards and shops encumbering the older townhouses — the gardens in the Marais were also redesigned *à la française* to give a new charm to this old section of Paris.

Although the most beautiful gardens are in the Hôtel de Soubise, the Hôtel de Rohan, the Hôtel de Lamoignon and the Hôtel d'Aumont, all the gardens have square lawns bordered with flowers and framed by

In winter the fountains are empty but it is not unusual to see a peaceful reader seated in the hollow of their curves, waiting for a furtive ray of sun (above). Oak, chestnut, yoke-elm, lime and ash trees are reflected in the ponds of Saint-Cloud (facing).

sumptuous eighteenth- or nineteenth-century buildings. They have become public monuments: the museum of the history of France (Hôtel de Soubise); the Seine Tribunal (Hôtel d'Aumont); and the historical library of the city of Paris (Hôtel de Lamoignon).

Despite their beauty, the Parisian gardens of the baroque, classical and rococo periods — designed according to the rules laid down by artists such as Boyceau, the Mollets, Le Nôtre, Desgots or Leblond — are no longer what they once were. Frequently redesigned, either because of urban development or the impoverishment of their vegetation, they have been subjected to the hazards of time and the myriad changes casually wrought by the dictates of fashion. Le Nôtre, for example, had no compunction about changing the layout of the Tuileries Gardens as soon as he was put in charge of them. The original ground plan, designed by two Italian masters, Tarquin and Carnessequi, was checkered, and included a maze, a tile factory (thus the name "Tuileries") and a fabulous grotto built by Bernard Palissy. Le Nôtre merely followed the example of his illustrious predecessors, Claude Mollet the Elder and Boyceau — who had already completely redesigned Catherine de' Medici's gardens — by adding box-edged beds, and above all, by sectioning it with a central walk bordered with slightly asymmetrical motifs to increase the impression of variety.

There is a lesson to be drawn from the freedom with which these artists handled the past. The present dilapidation of the Tuileries and their inclusion in the new "Grand Louvre" project, which implies a total reconstruction of the gardens, poses a problem: should conservative opinion prevail? In the name of "fidelity" to Le Nôtre, should his work be reconstructed identically, even though Le Nôtre frequently modified his own work (as can be seen in a 1671

engraving)? Or perhaps Le Nôtre's example should be followed and the genius of this great artist reinterpreted in modern terms.

In the wake of an international competition organized by the Ministry of Culture and based on a report by Monsieur Simonet-Langlart, the second option was judiciously selected. "Most of the trees are either sick or too old," explains Luis Benech (one of the winners of the competition). "Le Nôtre's design was modified too often; it can not be restored without taking into account the fact that the entire environment has changed." This artist is associated with a talented young architect, Pascal Cribier, who has a wonderful sense of space, and — since the results of the

Classical in composition, the Jardin de l'Intendant has monochrome and carefully designed flower beds for each season, set around the statue of Mansard (above).

and artists of the seventeenth and early eighteenth centuries, and above all, by André Le Nôtre, whose career and production surpassed those of all the artist-gardeners of his period.

Descended from a line of gardeners who had worked for the aristocracy of France, André Le Nôtre worked at his father's side and developed a solid practical knowledge of the métier. But on the recommendation of Boyceau, the young man studied geometry, arithmetic, drawing and architecture, and became an intellectual artist. Thus he often visited the studio of Simon Vouet, who was Louis XIII's painter, where he met Le Brun, with whom he later collaborated in the creation of Vaux-le-Vicomte and Versailles. He also studied treatises on perspective, probably including the one by the great geometer Gérard Desargues, who had worked for Richelieu as an engineer. To widen his artistic horizons, he traveled through Italy and Turkey as far as Constantinople, bringing back drawings of antique gardens designed by Greek artists for the Byzantine emperors.

By the age of twenty-two, André Le Nôtre was already "the first gardener for *Monsieur*, the king's brother" at Luxembourg; at only twenty-four he was nominated "master gardener to the king" for the "two plots facing the large pavilion at the Tuileries," a post in which he succeeded his father.

Le Nôtre inherited Claude Mollet's realm when he married into this brilliant dynasty of royal gardeners. Claude Mollet the Elder raised French gardening to the heights of its preclassical beauty. He enriched the checkerboard layouts with a multitude of ornaments th it can still be seen in the flowering sundi ils that decorate the lawns of Paris and all the towns of France. According to Claude Mollet, every garden should have flower beds, lawns and woods

competition were announced — with a well-known landscape designer, Jacques Wirtz. This is a promising team for a successful garden, but many years must pass before the results can be confirmed: the definitive project must be established and the work finished, and this is without even taking into consideration the time required for the plants to grow and reach their ideal sizes and shapes, thereby completing the large garden. The current project (as of June 1991) is an attempt to unify the Cour du Carrousel and the garden with a planted terrace that will cross avenue du Général Lemonnier. Twelve clipped yew hedges will radiate from the Arche du Carrousel to a basin on the site of the former Tuileries Palace. The garden, redesigned by Cribier and Benech, will retain its current form. The "reserved garden" will be separated from the rest of the garden by the "moat" and retain its Second Empire style. The parterres and the octagonal basin by the "horseshoe" staircase will be restored in a minimalist style. The sections near the Seine will be kept in their current state pending a possible enlargement of the gardens to the banks of the Seine.

The fact remains that these gardens from the past conveyed a view of nature that no longer exists. This "geometric" concept was known and adhered to by all the intellectuals, scholars

The design of the garden at the Carnavalet Museum includes well-designed flower beds and a profusion of ivy.

divided by intersecting paths, and long, forked, tree-lined walks leading to a park or a hunting forest. Furthermore, the gardens should be decorated with bowers, topiary in the shape of animals or people, mazes, separate flowering plots, and edged beds with colored gravel and flowers. This gives an idea of how the Tuileries Gardens must have looked in 1637, when André Le Nôtre (who had already worked with Claude Mollet the Younger for seven years) undertook a modernization project.

He immediately applied the new resources offered by linear perspective. The application of its three principles (to choose a fixed point toward which all lines converge; to reduce the entire space involved to one single plane and frame; and to make parallel planes follow one upon the other) was not an easy task in view of the amount of space that had to be organized and balanced to achieve the illusion of order and perfection. He was far away indeed from the "Italian-style" gardens posited by *The Dream of Polyphilus*, an initiatory text published in Venice in the late fifteenth century.

Designing a garden was no longer a question of creating a mixture of illusion and reality. It had to be something other than a temple of greenery made up of trees planted like theatrical columns with hidden cages full of

songbirds (like Marie de' Medici's apiary in the Tuileries) or an artificial mountain spewing torrents of water into the main pond, like the one in the Tuileries in 1575. Le Nôtre dreamed of a garden that would extend to the horizon and include the sky itself. He created this effect in the Tuileries by dividing the garden with a wide walk that appeared to enter the distant forest beyond present-day Étoile.

To the eighteenth-century mind, infinity — like God, truth and mathematics — was to be found in the very substance of nature. Art had to recreate the profound, vertiginous infinity that so obsessed Pascal, and everything in a garden had to participate in producing that effect. The palace and the surrounding park had to be an ordered element within the greater geometric entity that was formed, not by nature in the raw, but by the hidden truth of nature as designed by her Creator.

Yet French-style gardens are not merely gardens drawn with a slide rule, as has so often been suggested. Their geometry aims at a beauty that is magnificent, at a voluptuousness that fulfills the eye and the soul. These classical gardens were illuminated by numerous vistas, reflected in shimmering water in ponds, basins, waterfalls, cascades and jets, and balanced by trees that, like statues, define space. They had their own special magic and, although they were encompassed in an austere mathematical framework, they were meant for parties and pleasure.

The Tuileries, Luxembourg, Palais-Royal, Sceaux and Saint-Cloud, despite the fact that a number of these gardens were designed much later than the *Grand Siècle*, still convey this French spirit. This can be seen in the lightness of the main alley and the octagonal pond in the Luxembourg, or in the Palais-Royal, where the emptiness underlines its geometry. Sceaux — by an incredible act of

To see the ornamental fountains at Saint-Cloud, you must wait for the attendants. As in former times, they arrive with their gigantic keys and open the sluice gates of the fountains for an hour or two (above). Numerous plinths at Saint-Cloud are devoid of their statues. They were removed during the night of a violent storm in February 1990 (facing).

faith — once again reveals its vast cruciform composition, augmented by the long stretches of water and neat lawns; and the cascades and stonework set in the hilly grounds of Saint-Cloud retain a solemn grandeur.

Nevertheless, the original classical foundations of all these sites have mostly disappeared, partly because of the destructive upheavals of history, but also because it has become impossible, even for the State, to maintain gardens such as these. The cost of qualified personnel would be prohibitive, and the protection they would require does not accord well with the principles of democracy. During the reign of Napoleon I, the neoclassical architects Percier and Fontaine pruned and completely refurbished the Tuileries on the rue de Rivoli side. During

the Second Empire, the gardens almost became a landscaped park. Yet the Luxembourg Gardens were altered more than any other; since the garden was first designed, it has rotated ninety degrees around its main axis, and the shape and character of the park have been entirely transformed.

When the Luxembourg Gardens were first created, they were limited to the south by the Chartreux Monastery, and Boyceau cut a central walk running from east to west, parallel with the axis of the palace. In 1872, the eastern end of the gardens was parceled out. Ten acres were sold and the rue de Luxembourg, now rue Guynemer, was created. Two famous walks were lost: the Vallée des Philosophes — where Rousseau, who was staying in the Hôtel Saint Quentin, used to

The statues in the Luxembourg Gardens sometimes have an unexpected candor, giving off an opaline glow amid the green shadows of the branches.

walk every morning, and the lovers' walk, the allée des Soupirs. The nationalization of church property a few years later led to the expropriation of the greater part of the Chartreux domain. The Directoire, then the Empire, were therefore able to commission the architect Chalgrin to create a new vista, 1,400 meters long, running from the palace to the Observatory. With a new north-south orientation that faced the palace, the transformed Luxembourg Gardens were immense, for their southern edge reached almost as far as the boulevard Montparnasse. With the Senate's reputation for wisdom, power and conservatism, the affair should have ended there. But this extension of the major public garden on the left bank did not survive the speculative pressure of the Second Empire. After much violent argument, Baron

Haussmann prevailed, and he took land from the gardens to widen the rue de Vaugirard, to open the boulevard Saint-Michel and to create the rue de Medicis, turning the grotto into a fountain. Then, in 1865, he parceled and sold off the botanical gardens and the nursery.

When the Imperial decree authorizing these changes was published, Napoleon III and the Empress Eugenie were booed by the public at the Odéon. Petitions were gathered, in vain, even though one included some 12,000 signatures. The Senate remained silent and the emperor did not fire the baron; he agreed only to preserve the avenue leading to the Observatory designed by Chalgrin. The rue Auguste-Comte was built, and the Luxembourg Gardens were reduced to their present size. Yet this act also contributed

In the early morning at the Luxembourg Gardens, the jays in the oak trees are busy stashing food in their hiding places.

to the gardens' restoration, and today they offer the unique aspect of being two gardens in one: the classical garden near the palace and the landscaped English-style garden from the second half of the nineteenth century.

When walking around these gardens, where every path, flower bed and tree is a reminder of a major event or an anecdote in the history of France, it is impossible not to reflect on the various groups of people who frequented, or still frequent these parks, and on the different uses made of these spaces.

Here we are, on a bright sunny Sunday, in the Parc de Saint-Cloud. Laughing children chase across the wide lawns. Fathers dressed in track-suits play football while mothers, lying on beach towels, work on their summer tans. Farther along, picnic cloths have been spread under the shade of the lofty trees and bottles are being brought out of portable iceboxes, and, still farther, some people are busy around a pond where miniature motorboats are lined up at the starting post. With these peaceful family pursuits in view, it is hard to picture those ladies of earlier times, tight-clasped in their rich gowns, leaning on the arms of bewigged, powdered and patched dandies, gossiping about the king's latest craze as they strolled.

Winter visitors to Sceaux tend to linger in the Pavillon de l'Aurore while their children play on the black- and white-tiled perron near the entrance. Outside, the water in the canal lies icy and subdued; the sun pierces it without a ripple as it sets behind the Dutch limes; the grassy fields shine delicately as they slowly blend into the indistinct mass of the misty ground. In summer, visitors stand in wonder before the classical beauty of the incredible spectacle of the waterfalls. The sun burns down on the vast lawns and families take refuge in the shade of the trees. A festive feeling overwhelms the park.

In the Tuileries, people line up on the rue de Rivoli side to ride the ferris wheel, while by the Seine, men young and old perch on the walls like statues of flesh and blood offered for sale, hoping for an amorous adventure. Love — ugly, beautiful, happy, sad, freely given or venal — has always haunted Parisian gardens, but the Tuileries have the longest and most persistent tradition.

No sooner had the river side of the Tuileries been roughed out (on the orders of Catherine de' Medici), then occupied by tile-kilns, than the worldly, even licentious, vocation of the garden was established once and for all. Sauval, one of the first historians of Paris, wrote in the eighteenth century that if the hazel and cypress trees lining the paths that crisscrossed the gardens could speak, they "would tell us of gallant adventures that we know nought of." Though the queen never lived in the palace, preferring her mansion at Soissons, Henry IV did, staying in the Louvre until his assassination on the Pont-Neuf, above the square that now bears his nickname, the *Vert-Galant* ("the ever-young seducer"). When Louis XIII enlarged the gardens with a plot of land ostensibly belonging to one of his courtiers, it immediately became one of the most popular spots in Paris. Craftsmen and artists moved in, followed by *guinguettes*, or open-air dance halls. When Nicolas Poussin acquired a small property by the river, he described his paradise as an "absolute little palace on three stories, fully furnished, with a courtyard, an outhouse, a large, fully productive orchard and views on all sides." The small mansion occupied by Boyceau and later by Le Nôtre was probably equally pleasant. In any case, the changes made to the Tuileries by the master of the French style did not in any way alter the activities that went on there. In *Le Menteur*, Corneille had his Dorante say, at the time of the *Fronde* (1648-1653 rebellion) and the *Grande Mademoiselle* (Louis XIII's niece):

The elegant yews at Saint-Cloud have revived the art of topiary, long abandoned in Parisian gardens.

"But, since we are now in the Tuileries
The haunt of nobs and gallantries,
Tell me: do I look well as a gentleman?"

Why did the golden youth of the *Grand Siècle* come here? To have fun, of course. More than fun, in fact, if the memoirs of a certain aristocrat are to be believed, in which he confides that the height of dissipation was to be locked inside the Tuileries for a night of orgies.

It may have been the scandalous reputation of the gardens, rather than the damage that so many people could cause, that almost led to the closure of the Tuileries when the court moved to Versailles. It was of course a notorious Puritan, Colbert, who suggested that it be closed, and it took all the persuasive eloquence of Charles Perrault, author of *Peau d'Ane* and *Barbe-Bleu*, to make him abandon the idea.

The Revolution and the First Empire, however, did put a temporary stop to the licentiousness of the Tuileries. Too much blood had flowed along the terraces during the rebellions of July 1789 and August 1792, and on the Place de la Concorde where Doctor Guillotin's sinister invention worked nonstop. Yet the worldly vocation of the garden, by then opened to those who had been called "the populace" just a few years earlier, was revived. Crowds pressed in

on November 26, 1783 to watch the brothers Charles and Robert Montgolfier's balloons rise and the *Fête de l'Etre suprême*, staged by the painter David on June 8, 1794; and later, the festivities surrounding the coronation of Emperor Napoleon drew even more people.

With the arrival of the romantic era, the Tuileries (separated during the Restoration into two sections, one for the court and one for the public) once again became a place of pleasure, although it never reached the level of debauchery and fraud that was rampant in the Palais-Royal. But from morning to nightfall, it was the haunt of fashionable youth, ardent about love, art and politics.

It took the Second Empire, a fashion for the Champs-Élysées and, above all, the Bois de Boulogne, to deprive the Tuileries of its role as the open-air theater of Paris's worldly, political and intellectual life. Furthermore, the palace was burned down during the Commune, leaving a bare space between the garden and the nearby Louvre. Despite many attempts, no one has yet managed to recreate a proper transition between the two.

It is remarkable that the Tuileries, ill-treated, occupied by often mediocre statues and Maillol's sculptures, crossed with unkempt paths (sometimes badly tarred), and overrun by equally unkempt vegetation, should have retained any of its former beauty. The planned renovation should bring about the renaissance of this lovely and historic garden.

The Luxembourg Gardens are the opposite of the Tuileries. For many centuries they have been a haven on the left bank for children's games, walks, amorous pursuits and intellectual meditations. Except for the interlude of the Regency during Louis XV's minority, and the more dramatic one of the Revolution during which the palace was used

Busy in summer, the man who rents out small boats in the Tuileries will temporarily abandon his trade in the autumn, for lack of clients.

as a prison, the character of the garden has changed little. This peaceful aspect of the Luxembourg Gardens increased during the nineteenth century and the calm beauty of its walks and secret groves attracted poets. Baudelaire, born on the rue de Hautefeuille, was particularly fond of the gardens, and used to walk there with Jules Janin and Théodore de Banville. It is easy to understand why Victor Hugo, who knew the gardens from his childhood spent at the Feuillantines boarding school, had Marius, Cosette and Jean Valjean meet there in *Les Misérables*.

Anatole France's childhood memories, written fifty years after *Les Misérables*, concur with Hugo's impression. They are as fresh and clear

as if they had been written yesterday, as if time stood still in the Luxembourg Gardens. "I am going to tell you what the wild skies of autumn yearly remind me of. . . . I am going to describe what I see when I cross the Luxembourg Gardens in the early days of October, when it is a little sad and more beautiful than ever; for it is the season in which the leaves fall one by one onto the white shoulders of the statues. What I then see in these gardens is a little boy who, hands in his pockets and satchel on his back, hops toward school like a sparrow. My thoughts alone perceive him, for this little boy is a shadow; he is the shadow of *me* as I was twenty-five years ago. . . ."

Although he is now somewhat forgotten, in the early twentieth century Anatole France epitomized the progressive humanism that reigned in the Latin Quarter. It was at this time that the Luxembourg Gardens became fully integrated into the life of the "quartier," situated among the universities (Sorbonne, Polytechnique, Mines and Normale Supérieure), literary cafés such as the Closerie des Lilas — of which Baudelaire was already an habitué — the Capoulade, the Taverne du Panthéon, the Balzac and the Soufflot, and student dance-halls such as the Bullier and La Chaumière. Leconte de Lisle and François Coppée, Anatole France's colleagues at the

Students meet each other in the Luxembourg Gardens to read, to prepare for their exams or to whisper together (top). "I come and work in the Luxembourg Gardens because the light there is resonant and sibyline," confides a young painter (above).

painted by Manet, games of bowls and even the old-style tennis known as the *Jeu de Paume*. Finally, although the greenhouses are not open to the public, the horticultural school, or Cours de Luxembourg, carries on the tradition of the old Chartreux Monastery by enrolling over four hundred students a year.

Fragile, subject to the whims of history and fashion, vulnerable to climatic catastrophes and pollution, the great royal gardens of Paris have suffered greatly. Once entirely baroque or rococo, parts of them are now landscaped. Elements of the French style that remain, like the box-edged beds — where they have survived — are mostly restorations carried out in the style of the early twentieth century by master-gardener Achille Duchêne. Nevertheless, as they stand, their beauty continues to enchant us, proof that far from being a minor art, the art of gardening was, and still is, an essential part of French culture.

Did not the aging Le Nôtre receive the unique honor, reported by an almost incredulous Saint-Simon, of receiving a chair with royal bearers from the hands of Louis XIV himself, to enable him to visit his gorgeous gardens one last time?

library of the Senate, went to the Luxembourg Gardens because they lived in the neighborhood, while the starving Hemingway went there to kill pigeons for his dinner. Robert Brassillach, Roger Martin du Gard, Paul Nizan, Raymond Aron, Jean-Paul Sartre and Simone de Beauvoir frequented the east side of the gardens near the terraces on which Georges Pompidou and Léopold Sédar Senghor were photographed as students. Since the 1970s, however, when many of the universities were moved out of the Latin Quarter, the Luxembourg Gardens have somewhat lost their mythical place in French culture. But the intellectuals remain faithful, and it is not unusual to come across a well-known essayist exercising near the tennis courts, under the directions of a painter who also owns a literary café in Montmartre.

The west side of the gardens is the domain of children. Since the thirteenth century, it has offered all sorts of amusements: wafer, cornet and coconut sellers, pony traps, miniature sailing boats, merry-go-rounds and stalls selling delicacies and toys. André Gide, once a schoolboy at the nearby École Alsacienne, has left us a detailed inventory of these stalls: marbles, tops, liquorice sticks, pink or white tubes of aniseed, paper theaters, puppets of all kinds. For adults, there is a bandstand

Elderly people often escape their solitude by talking to the birds in the Luxembourg Gardens (top). Meanwhile, children swing energetically while waiting for the puppet theater to open (above).

*The bandstands return to life with the arrival of spring.
In the Luxembourg Gardens, fanfares, symphonic orchestras and jazz
musicians perform (top). Not far away, the Vialla café,
remarkably well restored in a 1930s style, has rediscovered its former
charm (above). The sculptures in the Square Georges Cain
in the Marais are there on temporary loan. Dawn, which belongs
to the Louvre, is the work of one of the
sculptors of the Parc de Versailles (following page).*

2

ROMANTIC
GARDENS

With the infinite variety of styles found in Parisian gardens, who would be tempted to compare Parc Monceau with Bagatelle? What could be more different than these two superb parks in their current state?

The Parc Monceau, inside the city, is eminently bourgeois. It is surrounded by opulent private houses built during the Second Empire and sheltered from the bustle of the boulevards by the tall wrought-iron gates that close off the avenues named after painters: Velazquez, Murillo, Rembrandt, Ruysdaël and Van Dyke. Threaded with elegant walks around generous lawns planted with ancient trees and dotted with statues of Chopin and Maupassant, Ambroise Thomas and Edouard Pailleron, the park and its neighborhood are redolent of good breeding and exude an aura of luxury. The powerful aura of the banks, the nouveaux riches, and the Stock Exchange impregnates the air, trees and stones of this distinguished park.

In comparison, the Bagatelle appears graceful and charming. Set in the Bois de Boulogne — instead of the stone-clad environment of the Parc Monceau — the Bagatelle consists of a series of gardens set in a landscaped area that is, in turn, surrounded by the vast greenery of the man-made forest. In early spring, when the irises, crocuses, hyacinths, scillas and narcissi spring from the grass, the gardens take on the colors of an impressionist painting. The sound of singing birds filters through the leafy trees while the blooming trellises in the rose garden compose fragrant poetry.

When the sun sets over the balustrade, the tawny owl awakens; the Parc Monceau has the greatest variety of birds in Paris.

there in the Bagatelle, dazzled by the profusion of daisies and jonquils and flowering fruit trees; there were whole beds of red tulips, heavy-headed, high lilac hedges, and enormous trees. I read Homer beside a stream: little ripples of water and great blasts of sun were playing on the rustling leaves. What sorrow so great, I wondered, that it could remain impervious to the beauty of the earth?"

When they were created, Monceau and Bagatelle represented models for a new kind of "pleasure garden," adapted to the changing tastes of the late eighteenth century. They were designed to be picturesque and to please the landscape painter.

The Bagatelle has none of the luxuriant aspect of Parc Monceau. Yet it offers a consoling freshness. Simone de Beauvoir, in *Memoirs of a Dutiful Daughter*, wrote: "I smelt the fragrance of freshly cut grass as I wandered

Both began as "Follies," both were built in the decade preceding the French Revolution

The narcissus of Bagatelle. In the first flush of spring, the bulbs form multicolored carpets, flowering after the crocuses, grape hyacinths and snowdrops (top). Mixed in with the wild grass, the Bismarck hyacinths perfume the alleys with their elegant fragrance (above).

on two very similar plots of land (just under twenty acres), each was purchased by a prince of the blood — the Comte d'Artois and the Duc de Chartres — and both were then in the countryside. Although this may seem odd given the present-day city limits, the "Folie Monceaux," originally called "Folie de Chartres," was outside the walls of Paris, on a plain that extended as far as Clichy — reputed to be very good game country.

This relatively remote location was necessary if the Duc de Chartres was to define his new property as a *folie*. Contrary to general opinion, the term "folly" at that time did not designate an extravagant domain or a frivolous purchase: the term came from the Latin *folii*, plural of *folium*, meaning leaf. Although the etymology of the word may seem strange today, it was not considered unusual at the time, because every wealthy person — in other words, anyone likely to follow fashion and acquire a folly — was supposed to read, write and speak Latin. Its meaning was closer to our modern "countryside" — in the sense of a "weekend property" — and to be qualified as such, it had to be outside the city. Thus it was not a *hôtel particulier* (private house), which would have been inside the walls of Paris, nor was it quite a château, in that the real or pretended aristocracy of the late eighteenth century claimed to prefer the "simple" to the "ostentatious."

The personalities of the Duc de Chartres and the Comte d'Artois, however, could not have been more dissimilar. The Duc de Chartres, owner of Parc Monceau, was a liberal, an anglophile and a Freemason, even though he was married to Louis XIV's great-granddaughter. Exiled in the early 1770s for his anti-totalitarian beliefs, he became the Duc d'Orléans in 1785. He was granted the name Philippe Egalité by the Paris Commune because of his revolutionary sympathies, and he joined his friend Mirabeau on the benches of the Third Estate. Father of the future King Louis-Philippe, this open partisan of the Enlightenment so sincerely hated despotism that he even voted for the death of his cousin, King Louis XVI (although this gesture did not save him — he was guillotined in 1793). Immensely rich, thanks to the innovative administration of his property learned from the Physiocrats, the Duc de Chartres was a "gentleman philosopher" with a taste for the "beauties of Nature" and, therefore, for the art of gardening, as is amply proved by his superb properties in the Palais-Royal and at Neuilly.

The Comte d'Artois, future Charles X, was ten years younger than the Duc du Chartres and epitomized the old regime at its most extreme: despotic, arrogant, selfish, pleasure-seeking, unintelligent, ill-educated and convinced that he deserved the privileges of his rank, his only excuse was his foolishness and a desire to impress. His every whim was realized at any cost. Bagatelle, for example, was created because of a 100,000-franc bet with his sister-in-law Marie Antoinette. He claimed that he could build a folly in a matter of weeks, and, to the horror of some of his peers, he set about it with a vengeance.

"A few days before our departure for Fontainebleau, our Lord of Artois decided to demolish a little house he owned in the Bois de Boulogne, called Bagatelle, and build, decorate and furnish a new one, merely to give a party for the queen when the court leaves Choisy to return to Versailles. Everyone thought him mad to attempt such an undertaking in the space of six or seven weeks. Nevertheless, he managed to build it, by employing 900 men who worked day and night.

"The most incredible part, however, is that finding himself to be short of materials,

The Bagatelle Garden contains admirable magnolias like the grandiflora which in July produces enormous white flowers with a citronella scent.

especially cut stone, lime and plaster, his lordship ordered patrols of Swiss Guards out onto the highways to seize every conveyance transporting these goods. Although they were paid for at once, most of the materials had already been sold to others, and this act was so outrageous that it angered the people.

"It is inconceivable that the king would countenance such irresponsible behavior, and, unfortunately, it is generally believed that it could not have be possible unless sanctioned by the queen." (Comte de Mercy-Argenteau, letter to Maria-Theresa of Austria, November 19, 1777.)

This senseless bet, of course, involved only the new building, because no amount of capriciousness on the part of the owner could have made the gardens grow in so short a time. It is a delightful little manor house designed by François-Joseph Belanger, who later produced the Wheat Exchange. He began the design of the gardens by laying out French-style lawns along the axis of the hastily built manor, in harmony with its rococo-Palladian style. But tastes had changed and Marie Antoinette, despite her indifference toward Rousseau and the philosophers of the Enlightenment, had become enamored of the pastoral delights of the grottoes, winding paths, bridges and waterfalls of her new garden at the Trianon. The Comte d'Artois, not to be outdone, decided to abandon Belanger's plan and, in order to make the results of his bet even more brilliant, he hired the Scottish master-gardener, Thomas Blaikie, to design the park.

Although only in his mid-twenties, Blaikie (1750-1838) was already renowned for having pioneered a new style in gardening. He was also a reputed botanist and had considerably enriched the famous collection of the Upton Gardens, Essex. The invention of the

"picturesque" or "landscaped" style of gardening was probably justifiably ascribed to a Frenchman, Charles-Rivière Dufresny, but Blaikie, who was to work mainly in France, benefited from the anglophilia of the times and from the reputation of his compatriots William Kent and Lancelot "Capability" Brown. These men had each, in turn, transformed the immense gardens at Stowe — created in the French style a century before — into an English-style landscaped park.

Blaikie was to spend six years overseeing the work on the Bagatelle, building a number of ornamental elements, including a shelter "like the ones the Indians build to protect themselves from wild animals" near the present entrance gates; a "philosopher's house"

At Bagatelle the flowers illuminate the surrounding urns and statues with a fragile and pervasive beauty (above). The luxuriant vegetation in the lily pond blossoms under the protection of a weeping beech, gnarled sophoras, and lime trees (facing).

The entire design formed a succession of picturesque landscapes with lawns, fields, large trees creating "forests" or "backgrounds," paths, ponds, streams and numerous constructions, and buildings inspired by history or the exoticism of distant countries.

Unlike Monceau, this marvel has not been completely destroyed, and surviving elements, though rare, can still be discovered by following the "river" that weaves past the small cascades and the reconstruction (much reduced in size) of "Palladio's bridge" that joins the cliff to the Gothic ruins.

in the Gothic style; a Palladian bridge; an "island of tombs" surrounded by willows, mock ruins and false antique statuary; and, lastly, on a "mountain" concealing an enormous ice-house, "Palladio's tower."

Nevertheless, this garden has lost much of its former glory. Perhaps the description of the "hermit's house" written by contemporary chronicler Luc-Vincent Thiéry in his *Guide*

Surrounded by remarkable trees, the Bagatelle château, the "folie du Comte d'Artois," was formerly reserved for elegant receptions (top). Their eyes fixed on the French-style garden, the two sphinxes are the mistresses of the château, the interior of which has just been entirely restored (above). A couple of ducks, who separate only when the female broods, wander around the Bagatelle islands. Their clipped wings keep them forever in the park (facing).

des Amateurs et des étrangers voyageurs à Paris best recaptures the spirit: "A narrow path leads to a grassy knoll in the background facing the spot where the river forms a little waterfall before entering the enclosure of the hermitage. . . . Leaving this delightful place, one crosses a bridge made of artfully grouped roots. Nearby, the river forms a large lake; small cascades tumble onto the rocks on the left side of this lake."

Lovely as Blaikie's gardens were, they were not well appreciated by their owner. The Comte d'Artois much preferred his manor house, whose motto, coined by Mademoiselle Rosalie Duthé, a dancer from the Opera, *parva sed apta* (small but practical), aptly describes it. But the gardener, who had a truly British sense of democracy, set about overcoming his master's indifference. In the *Diary of a Scotch Gardener*, Blaikie wrote:

". . . One day in the Morning arrived Mme de Polignac with some other ladys of honnour of the Queens to see Bagatelle and as the Compte was not up they desired not to call him; after walking and vewing the Gardens and asking me Many questons about the Compte and whether or not I was contented with him, I answered judiciously that I was not and that I never saw a more Lazier and a Man of less taste and that he had not once come to see the Gardens since he Lodged there; this gave no little Sport and Laughter to those Ladys who returned and told the Queen all that I had said. . . . Next Morning the great Company arrived and as I was walking with some of the noblemen the Compte D'Artois came out and seeing me at some distance called so that I went directly to him, so he asked me, 'Well, Blaikie are you not contented with me?' I told him no. 'Why so?' 'Because,' says I, 'there is no pleasure in working for you as I hardly know whether or not I please you as you never come to see the works after so much expences and as I wish to please you and that you should enjoy my works.' 'What,' says he, 'is it only that? I promiss I will come and see you oftener [*sic*].'"

A French-style garden flowers magnificently in front of the Orangery; this garden leads to an English-style garden, a unique feature of Bagatelle (top). Under the gaze of a small faun, an alley of arches opens up, deliciously scented in spring with langorous clusters of wisteria (above). The white "Empress's kiosk" constrasts with the brilliant colors of the roses at Bagatelle (facing).

The new style of gardens replaced the earlier French style that had dominated Europe for a century, and coincided with the thought and sensibilities of an age that was unconsciously preparing the political and industrial revolutions of the late eighteenth century, and the explosion of artistic and philosophical romanticism.

The "honest philosopher" had learned from Buffon and Linnaeus that nature, far from being restricted by geometry as the Cartesians would have him believe, was inexhaustible and variegated. Of course, it was possible to give nature some sort of order, with the help of classifications and encyclopedias, and there were physical laws such as the ones discovered by the great Newton, but these laws did not

alter the fact that the more it was studied, the more varied and irregular nature became. At the same time, the world's horizons were being enlarged by the exploration of new lands, and the ethics of display and total self-possession that had ruled behavior throughout the *Grand Siècle* were being replaced by a new sensibility — even sentimentality — in the name of the "natural" as opposed to the "conventional." Thus the ideological values and politics of absolutism were facing a crisis, even among aristocrats, while those of the English constitutional monarchy, personified by the "gentleman farmer," were becoming more and more popular.

Although this change in the intellectual climate had no effect on a man like the Comte d'Artois, secure in his beliefs of another age, he nevertheless superficially kept abreast of fashion. In this he was again the antithesis of his cousin, the Duc de Chartres, who was an ardent believer in the philosophy being put forward as the new universal model.

Nevertheless, the Folie de Chartres, begun in 1770, was a classically French-style garden, laid out by the architect Louis-Marie Colignon (one-time owner of the land) along the axis of a country house built in the style of Blondel. No sooner was it completed than the duke decided that he wanted a much larger, more modern park, and commissioned his master of ceremonies, Louis Carrogis (1717-1806), known as Carmontelle, to design it.

The choice was a good one; although Carmontelle was not a qualified gardener, he was a man of multiple talents: not only did he paint and draw, he was, like his predecessor Charles-Rivière Dufresny, a playwright and author. A scenic designer ahead of his time, Carmontelle was indeed a leader of that new style variously called "landscaped," "picturesque" or "Anglo-Chinese," in that his

A small cupid, pensive in front of the Impressionist beauty of the flower beds at Bagatelle (top). The elegant Orangery at Bagatelle harmonizes perfectly with the beauty of the park (facing).

aims were to compose varied "landscapes" that were attractive enough — both historically and geographically — to merit being painted.

Carmontelle, an artist-intellectual and theorist, was not impressed by the Puritan anglomania of the times that, as he said, neglected to "please women," who were nevertheless "the delight of society"; nor did he adhere to the apologia of a would-be "natural" Nature. In the *Prospectus* for his collection of landscape engravings of Monceau, he wrote, "Monceau was never intended to be an English garden; it is exactly as the critics have described it, every era and every place is gathered into a single garden. It is pure fantasy, born of the desire to possess an unusual garden created solely for pleasure,

and not in order to follow a Nation that, in the name of the natural, rolls every lawn and spoils nature by enclosing it everywhere in the narrow art of the unimaginative gardener." He went on to describe his plans for the garden, which was to have a Dutch landscape (including a windmill), an Italian vineyard, an Arab minaret, Greco-Roman temples (both ruined and intact), a Chinese garden with a "tilting yard" that formed a merry-go-round and a pagoda, a Tartar tent (complete with camel), and a Naumachia (a pond enclosed in a Roman arena for the staging of mock naval battles) around an obelisk carved with "all the hieroglyphs from Herodotus's obelisk." Carmontelle concluded, "Since it is possible to transform a picturesque garden into a land of illusion, why not do so? Illusions are our greatest pleasures and, since freedom guides

The Naumachia, an enigmatic colonnade at Parc Monceau, is from the tomb of the Valois at the Saint-Denis Basilica (above). In May, after the birth of the ducklings, the females take their offspring around the lake at Monceau (facing). Cleaned of its moss and parasites, the strange apparition of the Carmontelle Pyramid emerges in the Parc Monceau, guarded by caryatids of Egyptian inspiration (following page).

them, let Art design them; for thus we will never be far removed from Nature. Nature varies according to climate, let us also try to vary the climate, through illusion — or rather, let us make the spectator forget the climate around him by transposing the scene in our gardens as in an opera, and by reproducing the vistas of every era and land as a talented painter might do on a backdrop."

Was this ambitious plan carried out with a lack of technical expertise? Or was the anglophile and democratic Duc de Chartres influenced by criticisms of the "confusion" and baroque ostentation of this "land of illusion"? Whatever the reason, in 1783 Carmontelle had to step aside for Blaikie, who had already designed the gardens of the duke's property at Saint-Leu. From then on, until

Philippe Egalité was executed during the Terror — when Monceau became a "national estate" — the Scottish gardener concentrated on "naturalizing" the Folie de Chartres. He redrew the paths, planted trees and lawns,

*Limes, American honey locusts, Judas trees,
sycamore maples, figs, Eastern planes and copper beeches are among
the most beautiful trees in Monceau (above). Pansies and
daisies compose lovely parterres in the spring (above and facing).
Surrounded by private hôtels from the Second Empire,
Monceau has not lost its Proustian charm (following page).*

and enlarged the hothouses. On a surface area that had been enlarged by several acres and that included an involuntary *fabrique* — the Chartres Rotunda, a tollhouse built by Ledoux — he laid out a new landscape garden that was less theatrical, though more botanical and horticultural. His efforts were so successful that, to his great dismay, the chronicler Luc-Vincent Thiéry, writing on the eve of the Revolution, described the Folie de Chartres — which had become the Folie de Monceau — as an "English garden."

Like all the other Parisian follies (the Folie Saint-James in Neuilly, a small section of which, surrounding the enormous rock brought from Fontainebleau, survives; the Folie Beaujon at Étoile, and the Tivoli on the present site of Saint-Lazare station), Bagatelle and Monceau were swept away in the storm of the Revolution. Their *fabriques* fell into ruin and, although there were attempts to turn them into amusement parks or even, in the case of Monceau, into an open-air museum of "French monuments" under the Directoire and the Empire, they were rescued during the Restoration by their original aristocratic owners. But times had changed, and fashion with them. The taste for picturesque landscapes ornamented with curious constructions had been replaced by a

preference for romantic parks full of bushy trees and flowering beds. Above all, the inexorable advance of democracy made it inconceivable that parks, open to the public for over twenty years, would close their gates as if nothing had happened.

And so Monceau was abandoned, its neighborhood still on the outskirts of the city, until the westward expansion of the capital brought its fifty acres of prime building sites to the attention of the property speculators. By this time — the beginning of the Second Empire — most of the follies in Paris had been replaced by lucrative residential buildings, and Haussmann seized what he saw as a doubly profitable occasion.

He advised the city, which had become the owner of the park after the fall of Louis-Philippe, to sell half of the land to the Pereire brothers and to reinvest the money in the renovation of the other half, a project to be directed by his personal team of Alphand, Barillet-Deschamps and Davioud. Hence the Second Empire atmosphere of the park today, enclosed in a setting of private residences. Hence, too, the fact that only the Naumachia and the Egyptian Pyramid remain from Carmontelle's "land of illusions," to which one might add Ledoux's neoclassical tollhouse,

Parc Monceau preserves a few delightful kiosks from the late nineteenth century, along with a Renaissance arcade, a fragment from the old town hall (above). The sculptures placed throughout the park are tributes to great nineteenth-century figures: Maupassant, Chopin and Gounod (top). Other sculptures are set in the verdant lawns of the park (facing).

even though it was somewhat disfigured when the cupola was raised.

Nevertheless Monceau has retained its charm and is a much-loved park, because once inside, its silence is noble and voluptuously peaceful. Trees rise triumphantly from the vast lawns over which the rising sun spreads wide sheets of light. Everything in this tranquil park, still redolent of Proustian "nannies," breathes strength, richness and majesty: black pines, copper beeches, paulownias that in spring are covered in pinkish clusters of flowers, American honey locust trees, nettle trees, silvery lime trees, maples, a sycamore over thirty-five-meters tall, a Virginia tulip tree that turns magnificently red in the autumn, a fig tree, a seventy-year-old Oriental plane tree with a circumference of seven meters, the largest tree in Paris. While mallards fly overhead, the trembling reflections of the slender white Corinthian columns overlap those of the willow and the beech in the waters of the Naumachia, inviting visitors to meditate, not on the naval jousting of the centuries-old dreams of an exalted playwright, but on the astonishing variety of styles, the living mixture of the ages, and, above all, on the fragility of man's dreams and the melancholy of passing time.

Bagatelle, on the other hand, was relatively protected by the surrounding Bois de Boulogne. Admittedly, its new owners, Lord Seymour and later Richard Wallace, brought up in the school of the great English landscape artist Repton, raised the height of the pavilion, shortened the river and "rectified" the layout of the paths in Blaikie's picturesque park, finding them far too tortuous. Furthermore, they demolished many of the dilapidated *fabriques*, replacing them with antique-style statues that they considered to be improvements; these were in turn removed when the City of Paris expropriated the property in 1905. Nevertheless, the gardens were sufficiently well maintained during the nineteenth century that landscape gardener Jean-Claude-Nicolas Forestier, curator of Paris's west-side Promenades at the time, was able to restore Bagatelle's beauty by reinterpreting the park's original design.

Rather than attempting a faithful restoration that would have been inconsistent with modern tastes, Forestier harmoniously integrated two kinds of gardens: the sublime geometric rose garden, which bears his name, reminiscent of the classical garden designed by Bélanger; and groups of "landscapes." The variety of the "landscaped" areas was not dependent on the theatrical *fabriques* that Blaikie had used; instead, it was achieved through endlessly renewed compositions of different species of trees and flowers.

In 1774 Watelet gave the following definition of the picturesque, in his *Essai sur les jardins* (Essay on Gardens): "The picturesque, as the word itself implies, comes from painting. The painter assembles and places the objects that he chooses from Nature in a favorable aspect for his needs. The designer of a park should have the same aims, albeit limited by his means, for he will often face insurmountable difficulties, whereas the canvas lends itself to all the compositions of a painter."

In the days of Fragonard and Hubert Robert (who contributed to the creation of several follies, including Méréville and Ermenonville), it was natural that picturesque gardens should be composed of landscapes with ruins, grottoes, rocks and other fanciful *fabriques*. But at the beginning of the twentieth century, after the lessons of the Impressionist and Symbolist painters had been assimilated, it was just as natural that picturesque gardens should be marked by *japonisme* and by Monet, with whom Forestier worked and whose admirable garden at Giverny is known to all.

The mauve- and rose-colored wisteria flowers fall gracefully while the subtle scent of sweet peas fills the air along the length of the low walls at Bagatelle (facing). In their bower of pruned hedges, the roses of Bagatelle generously perfume the gardens. The sober lines of the rose garden are the product of the revived art of topiary (following page).

*Does the rose imitate the stone or is it the
stone that follows the undulating movement of the petals? (top).
This bas-relief by Nicolas S. Adam, lent to
Bagatelle for an exhibit on follies, has just been moved to
the Carnavalet Museum (above). At Bagatelle
the tender fountain of the Amours de Sudre offsets the Hispano-Moorish
style of the Iris Garden (facing).*

Thus, exploring Bagatelle today is like passing from a Renoir to a Seurat, or from a Manet to a Bonnard; as if every painter who loved color and light had gathered together to create a patchwork of perfumed paintings. After the allée de Longchamp that leads to the ceremonial entrance, a handsome walk edged with yew, forsythia and fern winds to the left between the Japanese pond and the maze and leads to the Orangery. This building shelters the orange trees in winter, along with Chile pines, pittosporums, camelias and phyllocactus.

Continuing to the left, midway between the Orangery's French flower bed and the perennials garden with its flowering walls, the path reaches the marvel of Bagatelle: the rose garden. In mid-June, at the height of its flowering, its geometrical layout is enchanting. Over seven hundred varieties of roses bloom in the light of early summer: *gallica, centifolia, canina, damascena, palustris, rugosa, sempervirens, leonida, phoenicia, pimpinellifolia.* They are white, yellow, pink or red; severely pruned or growing freely; proud standard roses or clusters tumbling around their foliage; in square or circular beds, in bowers, in arbors; new and old roses; and single or double flowers named after stars, queens and gardeners.

After passing the lilacs and Jean-Claude-Nicolas Forestier's medallion, the path arrives at the route de Sèvres in Neuilly, among the climbing plants, the asters, the dahlias, the clematis and the rambling roses; it then leads to the manor house of La Bagatelle itself. It is hard to believe that such a graceful building was erected in so short a time. The pond of the Nympheas, in the center of the French garden where topiary yews surround well-proportioned flower beds, is the main attraction in the summer. However, the walk is best continued along Blaikie's "river" to the

right, in the direction of the artificial lake of the Grand Rocher, in search of the vestiges of the Folie d'Artois. After that, visitors should explore the park at will, whatever the season; the enchanting colors of the lawns are dazzling. The brilliant landscape changes with every month: from the earliest days of spring, the pale green of the new grass is sprinkled with iris, primroses, narcissi, scilla of every color, while the sky above is pink and white with blossoming apple, plum, cherry, and rhododendron trees. After the tulips and hyacinths have flowered, the summer warmth brings forth great carpets of poppies, dahlias, lupins and roses, whose pinks and purples, saffron yellows and Parma violets harmonize with the luxuriantly blooming hortensias, tulip trees, magnolias and acacias. Finally, autumn blends the velvety pinks and ochres of the marigolds, chrysanthemums and asters with the red and yellow of burning leaves, against the background of the russet trees to the northeast that form the "sylvan forest."

The neopicturesque and neogeometric styles strike a different note in the gardens created by Albert Kahn in his property at Boulogne-Billancourt. A friend of Bergson, Kahn was a banker from the Vosges who dreamed of a universal brotherhood. To this end, he formed the *Cercle Autour du monde,* a circle in which people as brilliant and varied as Lépine, Rabindranath Tagore, the Countess of Noailles, Barrès, Jaurès, Chamberlain, Clemenceau, Poincaré, the Pasha of Marrakesh, Painlevé, Joffre, Lyautey, emissaries from the Emperor of Japan and the Maharajah of Kapurthala mixed in an atmosphere as hospitable as it was utopian.

Kahn realized the value of photography as a record of his times and an instrument of ethnographic research, and built up an immense collection of glass negatives of

*At Bagatelle, March is the best time to
admire the fields of flowers among the lawns: bulbs with intoxicating
scents, delicate mauve bifolia scillas and
yellow narcissus predominate, while the "Paperwhite," or white
narcissus, flowers in winter (above). In the autumn,
the foliage of the ginkgo biloba, also called the "Maidenhair Tree,"
is transformed into magical colors (following page).*

subjects ranging from Australian aborigines to Breton seaweed gatherers, that he called the "Archives of the Planet."

Besides these universal enterprises that made him a successor to the Encyclopedists of the eighteenth century, Albert Kahn, perhaps inspired by Bergson's vitality, was passionate about gardens. He therefore set about creating a series of landscapes that symbolized his vision of the world. In addition to planting several kinds of "forests"— including a "Vosgian" forest on the right side of the park, as a reminder of his childhood — he created an "English" garden with winding paths, a "French" garden with a greenhouse and rose garden, and a "Japanese" garden. This last included both a wet garden with exuberant vegetation and a Zen-style dry garden with a bamboo pavilion where, on certain afternoons, the tea ceremony was held.

Today the property, which belongs to the department of the Hauts-de-Seine, houses a museum of Nature and the Albert Kahn Archives. Despite their small size, the little-known gardens are exceptional. Sheltered behind high walls and nourished by the waters of the Seine, the vegetation flourishes. The trees in the miniature "forests" are tall and, although there are no wide vistas, the French-style flower beds form an elegant contrast with the English-style lawns.

The Japanese garden has recently been reopened. Albert Kahn's masterpiece had been left untended for so long that it lost its personality, so much so that in the end, Japanese authorities and businessmen were moved to take it in hand. However, instead of restoring the gardens, they redesigned them as a tribute to their creator. Visitors will not

A tea house remains in the old part of the Albert Kahn Japanese garden, where a traditional tea ceremony is still held.

find the garden that Kahn and his assistants put together so lovingly at a time when impressionism and art nouveau were under the influence of Japanese art. Japanese landscape-gardener Takano, who directed the work, created a new garden in which postmodern Japan celebrates an old Europe that has become exotic in its turn. A pyramid of pebbles symbolizes the birth of Albert Kahn. From it springs a stream representing his childhood that becomes a river and flows into a lake overhung by a bed of fuchsia, orange and carmine azaleas, which evoke the generosity of the banker. The river then leaves these brilliant surroundings, slips under two Japanese bridges and disappears.

Many other Parisian parks, gardens and even squares are equally picturesque, though less subtle. The woods of Boulogne and Vincennes are full of man-made lakes, waterfalls, chalets, grottoes, islands, fields and rivers set among those forests so dear to bourgeois romanticism. There are also obelisks,

The gravel walks in the Jardin Albert Kahn lead to the Vosges-style forest, where the heather flourishes luxuriantly.

pyramids and pseudo-Moorish *fabriques*; these are no longer fantasies in the style of Carmontelle, but rather reminders of colonial power. The Buttes-Chaumont, which successfully integrates the modern city into a hilly environment, sometimes looks like the landscapes in *Le Voyage de Monsieur Perrichon*, sometimes like the extraordinary worlds explored by Jules Verne.

The ruins of ancient Paris are often prominently displayed in many of the city's squares. Situated in the rue Payenne in the heart of the Marais, the Square Georges Caïn serves as storage space for the stone artifacts of the Carnavalet Museum that overlooks it. The piles of remains of lost monuments — fragments of broken columns, copings, curbstones, statues — frequently covered in

ivy or climbing plants, are as pleasing as a painting of ruins by Hubert Robert. Is it because time appears to stand still, or because these stones symbolize its passing?

The Square des Arènes de Lutèce owes its existence to the discovery, in the course of some roadworks in 1870, of a group of Roman ruins. Covered up through the centuries by the gardens of the many religious houses that were established around the Montagne Saint-Geneviève, the arena of the ancient Gallo-Roman city had been lost: Sauval, in his *Antiquités de Paris* published in the seventeenth century, placed them lower down the hill, toward the rue des Boulangers. For the Parisians, the discovery of the ruins on the eve of the war of 1870 was an exciting encounter with the past. Subscriptions were

The Arènes de Lutèce, an unusual amphitheater in the center of Paris, has exceptional acoustics and is used for summer concerts (above). The windows of the Carnavalet Museum offer a superb view of the Square Georges Cain and its spectacular sculptures, like the Sun relief (facing).

raised "to preserve this magnificent ruin at any cost and to finish its excavation," but the restoration of the site was only started twenty years later, under the supervision of Formigé, and completed in 1923. The Arénes de Lutèce is not, after all, the Coliseum, and its spectacular rehabilitation did not hold the attention of a novelty-loving public for long. Nevertheless, this dual-purpose edifice was impressively large: it included a podium and five *carceres* which housed the wild animals for the gladiator fights, a forty-meter-wide stage (with nine niches cut into it to improve acoustics), and steep tiers surrounding the oval circus. According to Jean Paulhan, "naval jousts followed the combats of the gladiators, and those of animals followed tragedies and comedies" before ten thousand spectators. Today a quaint monumental staircase links it to the small Square Capitan below it, while an outrageously twisted beech tree (over a meter in circumference for a height of two meters) dominates the theater. Seated on the tiers, students read in the morning sunshine. Children play in the sand pit or on the slide and, on the very spot where men killed each other twenty centuries ago, retired workers peacefully play at bowls.

The Square Saint-Jacques, the first Parisian

square created by Alphand and Barillet-Deschamps, was given special attention. Exotic trees with unknown perfumes were imported at great expense to form a setting for the tower that an architect, using a complicated technical manœuvre, had lifted up in order to set it on a neo-Gothic pedestal. But it almost seems as though the curse that lies over the church of Saint-Jacques-de-la-Boucherie — "any opposition church," according to Victor Hugo — made this historic square a victim of irreparable dilapidation. The restoration carried out at the end of the 1960s, with the pretext of renewing its vegetation, destroyed the lawns and settings of the garden, and imprisoned the shrubbery in stone and cement tubs. Despite these outrages, the fifty-two-meter tower built in 1522 by Jean and Didier de Felin saves what remains of the first Parisian public garden from disaster.

By the same token, what would Square Cluny be like without its Gallo-Roman ruins? A sad bit of greenery, it is the grassy result of unfortunate urban planning. But the thick arched wall that backs it — the remains of the Baths of Constance built at the beginning of the third century that housed "a palestra, a library, an art gallery and hot baths"— and its connection with the Cluny Museum give it a poetic charm.

*Resembling a Mayan temple, these stones from the excavations of the Arènes de Lutèce are at the end of a sumptous alley of sophoras (above).
The benches in full sunlight overlook the arena (above).*

An atmosphere that is both strange and contemplative surrounds the parochial vestiges of two small neighboring squares: Square Saint-Séverin, where there are a few ruins; and Square Viviani next to the church of Saint-Julien-le-Pauvre. One April day in 1920, this church was the pretext for one of the "excursions and visits through Paris" organized by André Breton and Georges Ribemont-Dessaignes during their dadaist period. Both squares demonstrate, as does the reappropriation of Ledoux's rotunda by the architect Bernard Huet in the new square in Place Stalingrad, that the "ruinous" picturesque can save even the dullest green space by transforming it into a landscape.

Although it has been long disparaged by architects and urban designers of the modern movement who perceived it as mere fallacious nostalgia, the picturesque is being revived today.

Freed from the fantasies of progress and the illusion of a clean slate on which to inscribe a radiant future, our age is relearning how to look at a multifaceted world, and to enjoy landscapes whose modernity comes from the past as well as the future, and from artifice as much as from formal purity. Every garden in Paris created in recent years includes a vine, curious *fabriques*, or some reminder of the site on which it is built. And each new park includes a symbolic tale that provides a clue to the site itself, as is the case with Parc de la Villette and the future parks of Bercy and Citroën.

*Beneath the chestnut trees, a dramatic double
stairway descends from the Arènes de Lutèce toward a small square (above).
In autumn, the leaves of the tulip trees possess a
flamboyant beauty that transforms the landscape of the Parc Montsouris (following page).*

3

TREES AND FLOWERS

A unique link has always existed between Paris and its surrounding natural beauty, but it was not until the Jardin Royal des Plantes Médicinales became the Jardin des Plantes (Botanical Gardens), followed by the influences of the First Empire and the Romantic era, that the planting began that transformed Paris into the city we know today.

The gardens in Paris, which add a floral exuberance to every neighborhood, are replanted several times between March and November to create fresh forms and colors to delight the eye. Tended by several thousand gardeners ranging from park directors to gardening apprentices, they are in a state of perpetual renewal. Close to 4,200 people are employed in the parks, gardens and green spaces of Paris, and several thousand civil servants take care of the five great national gardens of the Tuileries, Luxembourg, Palais-Royal, Museum of Natural History and Parc de La Villette.

Three times a year, 60,000 plants are distributed among the three main flower beds set in the 60,000 square meters of lawns surrounding the walk that leads to the central pond near the palace in the Luxembourg Gardens: autumn chrysanthemums are replaced by primroses, tulips, myosotis, stock and pansies that bloom under the new leaves of the chestnut trees and yoke elms, and summer brings forth a brilliant mass of dahlias, sage, geraniums and ageratums.

Paris, rising from the ground in a vertiginous series of streets, façades, staircases, courtyards, passageways, rich palaces, pilasters and columns, is one of the most stone-clad cities in the world. But for over two centuries, trees, plants and flowers have been added to the city's greenery, making it also the most wooded capital in Europe. Its gardens,

squares and flowering traffic circles add a luster to the movement of light over the stones. They are brightened by the greenery and colored into patches of red or purple that at sunset dissolve into a delicate pink.

Close to 500,000 trees representing eighty species and more than 300 varieties grow in Paris. Over two million flowers are planted in 45,000 square meters of beds: 884,000 spring flowers; more than one million summer plants; 146,000 winter ones. And, on June 20, 1990, the planting of the 500,000th rosebush in Paris was celebrated on the Champs-Élysées.

With the beginning of urban planning, alignment trees were planted along the streets,

The view from the Butte-du-Chapeau-Rouge, a typical 1930s garden, stretches far to the east (above). In the Bois de Boulogne, the "Papyrifera," or paper birch, stands out among the darker trees (facing).

Square Viviani, near the church of Saint-Julien-le-Pauvre, planted during the same period.

When all the open spaces in Paris, arranged by the gardeners and enlivened by the arrival of spring, display their beauty under the slate-colored sky, the composition is so subtle that it would be difficult to catalogue the contents for fear of leaving out the best elements.

The trees and flowers of Paris would probably be less varied had it not been for the *furor hortensis* which, after seizing England and Germany, spread to France in the early nineteenth century. Of course, long before the French romantic movement began, the gardens of the Marais were full of lilies, carnations, and red and white roses. The *courtilles* or large public gardens, such as the Temple, Saint Martin, Barbette and Boncelois on the outskirts of Paris, were country parks where, according to Sauval, "the bourgeois as well as the Templars and the monks of Saint Martin used to walk and take the air," and also drink the wine know as *vin de la courtille*, which, as he said, "was generally more pleasing to the eye than to the palate."

The Renaissance *orceads* flowered and bore their fruit in the "meads" of the Parisian hills. As for seventeenth-century gardens,

avenues and boulevards of the city. Although an ordinance was issued by King Henry II in 1552 for the planting and maintenance of trees, is was not until 1616 that someone, namely Marie de' Medici, planted four rows of elms along what is now the Cours-la-Reine. However, rows of aligned trees were widely used for the first time in 1670 when the first "boulevards" replaced the ditches and ramparts that had been built to protect Paris from the Comte de Nassau, an ally of Charles V. The results were judged to be so successful that a commemorative medal was struck bearing the inscription *Ornata et amplificata urbe*. Similar plantings were carried out along the wide pavements and side streets touching each main street. Many of the 85,000 alignment trees were planted during the last century and are now reaching their maximum age of 100 years. They are mainly plane trees (41%), chestnut trees (15%), sophoras (9%), lime trees (7%), maples (6%), acacias (3%), cedrelas (3%), poplars (1%) and elms (1%). As for the 400,000 forest-sized trees in the municipal parks and the woods of Boulogne and Vincennes, 65% of them were planted before 1900. There are a few ancient historic trees still growing in Paris, such as the false acacia planted in the early seventeenth century in the Jardin des Plantes (now reduced to a few shoots), and the one in

The chestnut trees in the Bois de Vincennes form vaults that keep the alleys cool in summer (top). The trees in Paris need attentive care to survive, and special protection is sometimes created for them (above).

In Paris, the trees are transformed into
gigantic bouquets in springtime — white or pink prunus,
chestnut trees with transparent leaves,
plane trees with monoecious flowers, and maples in bud.

supposedly austere and full of box-edged beds with traceries filled in with sand, black loam and even brick dust and metal shavings, Sauval wrote: "In numerous spots one can see great quantities of gardens planted with tulips, anemones, carnations and all sort of flowers, not to mention plants and medicinal herbs, for they are to be found in the Faubourg Saint-Marceau and the Faubourg Saint-Michel, in the Temple, in Montmartre and in almost every quarter of Paris and its outskirts."

However, these pleasure gardens belonged to a privileged group — nobles, churchmen or prominent merchants — and, rather than being intended for pleasure, they were showpieces in which every element was designed for the eye, not for feeling.

"Feeling": this was the key word which, along with the "self" in quest of a personal paradise, was to appear at the end of the eighteenth century and become of widespread interest during the nineteenth century. The "feeling for nature" engendered a desire for parks and forests in which exalted souls could escape their fetters. Rousseau immediately comes to mind, as does Chateaubriand. In his cosmic verse, the author honored the sap that gave birth to plants. About his property in the Vallée-aux-Loups, he wrote: "This place pleases me, I am fond of my trees, I have written them elegies, sonnets and odes. . . ."

This romantic love of trees explains the amazing quantity of trees planted in Paris and its outskirts under the First and Second Empires, while later on, the Symbolists would exalt "flesh" and "melancholy" in their use of the word "flower."

Viscount Chateaubriand and Empress Josephine actively embraced these movements, one thoughtfully but with small means, the other spontaneously and with access to the money of the State and experienced botanists, especially those of the Muséum.

Chateaubriand was busy laying out his park in the Vallée-aux-Loups while Empress Josephine Rose de Beauharnais was overseeing the creation of her gardens at Malmaison, in Rueil. Both were delighted by the "curious" plants in their gardens and parks, and they even exchanged rare shoots, as gardeners have done since the beginning of time: thus Viscount Chateaubriand received a red magnolia bush from the empress during a visit in 1811. The combined influences of science, travel and a certain sensitivity furthered the acclimatization of tropical plants and trees. Eucalyptus, hibiscus, amaryllis, camelia, a great variety of heather, myrtles, geraniums, mimosas, magnolias, cactuses, rhododendrons

The prunus in the Luxembourg Gardens are adorned with delicate pink or white flowers in spring (facing).

and various species of dahlias, peonies, tulips and double hyacinths entered French gardens during this period.

While Josephine was spreading her taste for flowers and the fashion for collecting them in the teaching gardens of Lyon and Marseille, Chateaubriand was transforming the Vallée-aux-Loups into a center of romanticism: "I was in a world of endless enchantment . . . donning a pair of clogs, I used to go and plant my trees in the mud, and wander up and down the paths visiting every little corner over and over again, hiding behind each patch of undergrowth to imagine what my park would look like in the future." And indeed, the author fashioned a park worthy of a landscape painter out of this uncultivated and tree-filled little valley. He bought the property on his return from a trip to the East in 1807, and divided his time between writing — finishing *Martyrs*, putting *Moïse* into verse and, above all, reviving the project he had planned in Rome after Pauline Borghese's death of writing his memoirs, which would result in his *Mémoires d'outre-tombe* — and designing the walks of a picturesque park where the trees reminded him of his travels in America, Italy, Greece, Spain and Palestine.

Fontanes, Joubert, Bérenger and women such as Madame de Récamier, de Duras, de Boigne and Marshall Junot's wife visited the writer. Lamartine, then aged eighteen, saw "a small man dressed in black with wide shoulders and a noble head" come out of the house, followed by a cat. "That was enough for our poetic superstitions," he was to write later in his *Courrier familier de littérature*.

As soon as Chateaubriand settled in the Vallée-aux-Loups, gossip and legends surrounding the writer were suddenly widespread. He found them amusing: "In Vienna. . . . they say that I lived all alone in a certain valley. . . .

My house was built on the island; when people wished to visit me, they had to blow a hunting horn from the opposite bank of the river (the river at Châtenay!). . . ."

Another story asserts that Napoleon, out hunting in the nearby woods, was so curious to see the retreat belonging to his illustrious opponent that, accompanied by an aide, he actually questioned the gardener Benjamin, after giving him some pieces of gold, and admired the belt of chestnut trees, the narrow winding walks and the exotic trees.

A cedar planted by Chateaubriand still stands on the boulevard Raspail, and his park and house in the Vallée-aux-Loups are now open to the public. Most of the trees that he planted so lovingly on the lawn facing the two wings of the house are still there: cedars, catalpas, tulip trees, weeping pines. Even Josephine's red magnolia still flowers magnificently in the park itself, under the shade of the chestnut trees, not far from the Velléda tower.

François René de Chateaubriand and Josephine de Beauharnais shared a taste for the exotic. The generosity of the empress has been mentioned; we will now explore her achievements, and how she created Malmaison, which became a marvelous example for other landscape-gardeners.

While Chateaubriand had a preference for trees, the empress loved flowers. Unable to build a palace to suit her tastes, she embellished the gardens instead, and had a hothouse designed along the lines of the one that had been recently built for the Muséum. She expanded her lands constantly: comprising 642 acres when it was purchased in 1799, it had grown to almost 1,800 at the time of her death in 1814. To a great extent the development of the park and the gardens of Malmaison were consistent with Napoleon's

In spring, the laburnum drop their langorous, sweet-smelling clusters of flowers.

plans to restore the great "French-style" royal parks in order to bolster his own prestige: "I want a straight, shady promenade," he told his architects. He wanted to make his capital "not only the most beautiful city that has ever been, but that will ever be . . . something colossal, heretofore unknown." When he learned from a historian that the parks' enclosures were a relic of the Middle Ages, the emperor decided to bring the age of enclosed gardens to an end, and opened up wide passages planted with trees. Paris, once stifled by a multitude of walled gardens, began to breathe at last. One entered the city through new vistas such as Neuilly or the park at Saint-Cloud, which would soon become part of the capital, while Saint-Germain, Versailles and Malmaison became its suburbs.

Josephine's taste for luxuriant vegetation and tropical plants, acquired during her childhood in the West Indies, must have contributed greatly to her efforts to create a new kind of landscape at Malmaison. Her passion for horticulture was such that it became fashionable. She began modestly, planting seeds sent from the West Indies by her mother. The work was later placed under the supervision of Morel and the botanical transformations were carried out according to the plans of two landscape-gardeners: Howatson, an English gardener who had worked on Monceau and Bagatelle before the Revolution; and Brisseau de Mirbel, a member of the National Institute, a familiar figure in the Muséum and a leading botanist of the eighteenth century.

Brisseau de Mirbel generously distributed plants and cuttings from Cherbourg to Nîmes, including Dax, Elbeuf, Saint-Sever, Nantes, Marseille, Lyon, and the Vallée-aux-Loups. For Malmaison, his friend, the gardener and explorer Félix Delahaye, contributed great quantities of seeds of tropical plants, a large herbarium and his personal knowledge of this new botany; other seeds were provided by the *Muséum*. The botanist Aimé Bonpland, who had explored Mexico and the banks of the Orinoco with the German scholar Alexander von Humbolt, was called to Malmaison: he gave Josephine some of the rare plants that he had collected during his travels.

Aside from the cedars (including the cedar planted to celebrate the battle of Marengo), the garden has catalpas, tulip trees, araucarias, black pines, Virgina cypresses, Chinese *Yukan* magnolias, eucalyptus and rhododendrons.

And finally, the flowers, the myriad flowers that the empress had studied, described and painted. The Malmaison archives contain instructions for gathering seeds, as well as

"The azalias formed a bush of coral," wrote Chateaubriand about his retreat in the midst of the trees in Vallée-aux-Loups (above).

*In the romantic universe of Vallée-aux-Loups,
the Lebanese cedars, the pines, the bald cypresses, and the Greek plane
trees admirably evoke Chateaubriand's voyages.*

entrance halls and conservatory drawing rooms. Newly installed elevators transformed the hierarchy of floors, and rooftops were turned into elegant gardens and greenhouses full of magnolias, tulip trees, Japanese plum trees, fruit trees and flowers in abundance: fuchsias, hortensias, althaeas, roses.

Modern Paris has succeeded in retaining a discreet beauty despite the *furor hortensis* of the beginning of the century; unlike other European capitals such as London or Vienna, Parisian vegetation is rarely showy. Occasionally, a half-open gate offers a glimpse of an interior garden of one of the aristocratic townhouses built on the religious enclosures of the past.

The large Parisian gardens and parks all have rare trees and delicate compositions of flowers, generally planted in wide borders around soft green lawns, rather than in beds.

On the other hand, the public squares, designed more for social than creative purposes, are tiny enclaves of greenery. The Department of Parks and Gardens of the City of Paris has been working to improve them over the last few years. They are administered by one or two gardening overseers assigned to one of the eight departments that are responsible for the squares, woods and gardens of Paris. The head of the department chooses, with the approval of some twenty assistants, the annual floral decoration for the squares and gardens under his responsibility; he then oversees the planting and the annual, biennial or triennial rotation of all the lovely cameos in red, yellow and blue that adorn the city. Each department employs

*Small daisies, nasturtium, carnations, ranunculus
and marguerites are reappearing in Parisian gardens (above).
In May, beneath the superb mauve clusters of
paulownia, or in autumn, when the chrysanthemum bloom,
the flower market on the Île de la Cité
adds a bright splash of color along the Seine (facing).*

200 to 300 people, ranging from the engineers in the public works departments to the occasional assistant landscapist and the secretaries. Plants are ordered from the greenhouses in Auteuil or from the tropical greenhouses in Rungis and, occasionally, from private suppliers.

Rhododendrons, azaleas, heather and even lavender are some of the first choices after annual plants like begonias or geraniums, bulbs like crocuses, hyacinths, daffodils and tulips planted in the lawns, or summer plants like pansies or cannas. But the rosebush remains the most popular plant in Paris.

Two lovely rose gardens grace the Paris region: L'Haÿ-les-Roses, a vast property overlooking

the valley of the Bièvre and the town of Bourg-la-Reine opposite the Parc de Sceaux, and Bagatelle. While L'Haÿ is considered to be the "archives" of the rose, Bagatelle is seen as the "showcase" for the rose.

When the City of Paris decided to create a rose garden at Bagatelle in 1905, Jean-Claude-Nicolas Forestier, the landscape-gardener who designed and constructed the garden, asked for the help of Jules Gravereaux, creator of L'Haÿ, who donated a great number of plants. The French-style rose garden of Bagatelle that extends in front of the Orangery contains some 9,000 rosebushes, and every year on the third Wednesday in June, the winners of the International New Rose competition are given a place of honor within the garden. On that day the most celebrated rose growers in the world meet in Paris with French rose grower Alain Meilland.

Jules Gravereaux, an enthusiastic amateur and rose collector, bought L'Haÿ when he retired in 1892. He had acquired so many roses by 1899 that he commissioned the architect and landscape-gardener Édouard André to design the world's first rose garden. Before this time, rosebushes were used to embellish garden walks and borders. Although Josephine conceived of the principle of a rose garden, she did not set aside a specific area for them in her rose-filled gardens.

While expanding his own fabulous rose garden, Jules Gravereaux, assisted by horticultural rose growers, assembled 350 *gallica* roses to recreate Josephine's rose garden at Bagatelle. He then duplicated it at L'Haÿ, using two flower beds separated by a path and covered by arches on which, as at Malmaison, the roses bloom between the collection of *gallica* ramblers and the unusual rosebushes in the garden of Far Eastern roses.

In summer, the baskets of bulbs, primroses and pansies at the Pré Catelan are replaced by mosaics of vivaciously colored flowers.

In addition, a rose "conservatory" has recently been built at Malmaison not far from the Cedar of Marengo, and visitors can now stroll among the empress's roses. The present layout, in the shape of an English flag, was taken from two watercolors (1806 and 1815) exhibited in the second floor of the house.

Jules Gravereaux's rose garden grows more beautiful every day. The marvelous "perfumed rose of L'Haÿ," still the standard for the International New Rose competition, was created by him.

During the 1960s, when flagstone and mineral gardens first appeared — such as the gardens along the Seine riverfront and the new gardens on boulevard Pereire — there was also an attempt to revive the floral garden. This resulted in the creation of a major new park, the Parc Floral de Paris in the Bois de Vincennes, on the site of the former military buildings, the Pyramide and the Cartoucherie. The landscaping team, led by landscape

Beneath the dome of L'Haÿ-les-Roses, a copy of Falconet's
Bather *is delicately enveloped by "Alexandre Girault" roses (top). The gallicas,*
the most rustic flowers of the rose garden, release a delicious scent.
Until the eighteenth century, they were the only roses cultivated in the West (above).
Flower beds of large double roses, planted in this decorative area of
the rose garden, create interesting effects of color and perspective (facing).
The rose garden contains some of the beautiful
varieties planted during the creation of the garden (following page).

architect Daniel Collin, turned an area of seventy-seven acres into the largest green space created in Paris since the Second Empire.

The Parc Floral is designed to be a pleasure garden (with a large children's play area) and an exhibition area for an extraordinarily varied number of plants. It has a valley of flowers, a sculpture garden, a country garden and an iris garden; yet it is far from being poetic. It is, instead, an uncomfortable arrangement of garden shapes, walks, flower beds, rockeries, and waterfalls. Admittedly, its lack of soul is not due to incompetence; the valley of flowers alone — an undulating 30,000 square meters in which 100,000 plants flower each season — is a tribute to the French style of gardening. This reproach is not aimed at the gardeners

who maintain the park, but at those who designed it.

Although the park does contain some beautiful elements, the overall effect lacks a certain integrity. The colors are too artificial, the layout of the hills and ponds is too arbitrary, and the handsome statues of the Carré des Arts are lost among the imprecise shapes of the lawns. Nevertheless, the technical mastery of horticulture exhibited in the thematic pavilions is admirable.

A visitor leaving the eastern edge of Paris for the west side will find traces of this same belt of forest in the Bois de Boulogne. Anyone who loves floral gardens, and who is already familiar with Bagatelle and the Auteil greenhouses, will certainly go to the Pré Catelan to breathe in the scent of the Shakespeare garden and its theater

*In the heart of the Pré Catelan, the Shakespeare Garden
is a botanical masterpiece, created in 1952 on the initiative
of the Cultural Advisor to the British Embassy.
Carnations and lavender form the Mediterranean garden. Plays are
performed each summer in this delicate verdant theater.*

*Saxifrage, a dense and sophisticated moss,
flourishes amid the heather in the Shakespeare Garden.
A path follows the stream of Ophelia where
the orange day-lilies and marigolds flower in May (above).
Daisies delicately intertwine the steps
that lead to the waterfall and the Greek wood (facing).*

*The lovely peacocks in the Parc Floral are the object
of constant admiration (above). The iris is called "the poor man's
orchid" by the gardeners in this park; every year in
May the park displays more than five hundred varieties of this
delicately scented flower (facing).*

of greenery — the homage of the city of Molière to the greatest of modern playwrights. The garden consists of plants found in his plays: heathland from *Macbeth*, a fragrant Mediterranean island from *The Tempest*, a water garden strewn with ferns, yellow pimpernels and globe flowers from *Hamlet*, the Mediterranean woods from *A Midsummer Night's Dream*, and the Ardennes forest from *As You Like It*.

The lights shining on the water in the pond brings to mind Monet's *Nymphéas*. Through his paintings reflecting the colors of his garden in Giverny, he was able to lend, for a moment, these same colors to Paris.

Paris is also stippled with shades of pale wisteria, like those along the rue Berton that Apollinaire used to visit for pleasure, strolling along the old walls. One of these walls, below rue Raynouard, encloses the garden of Balzac's house; at the Hôtel Biron flourishes the wild rose garden where Rodin sculpted among the flowers while his friend Monet hung his canvases for their joint exhibition of 1889.

The gunnera manicata in the Parc Floral is a sumptuous tropical plant from Brazil. It likes water but cannot tolerate the sun (above). Right beside it, in the shadow and humidity, the German ferns blossom in a rosette shape (facing). Wide rows of plane trees, majestic in winter even without their foliage, lead toward the many treasures of the Jardin des Plantes (following page).

4

BOTANICAL GARDENS

The first botanical gardens appeared during the sixteenth century in Padova, Italy, and in Montpellier, France, even though some aristocrats already had gardens containing "rare plants" and "curiosity cabinets." In Paris, a 1515 map of Tapisserie provides the first evidence of a "Royal Garden." The more detailed Belleforest map of 1575 shows a small enclosure at the western end of the Île de la Cité (on what is now Place Dauphine), divided into four sections, the work of Jean Robin. In addition to importing rare plants from Holland for the ladies of the court — always eager for new patterns for their embroideries — and supervising this enclosure, Robin was responsible for a block of gardens outside the walls of the city that belonged to the medical school, the "Lyceum Philosophal," which attracted many visitors who came for peaceful strolls among the "curious" plants. On the nearby Butte Coypeau, close to a windmill and enclosed by a hedge of thujas, lay a prosperous vineyard. This hillock was to become the "mountain" with its Grand Labyrinthe in the Jardin des Plantes. A medicinal garden was soon added by Nicolas Houël to "give great delight and adornment to the city of Paris." In 1630 Guy de la Brosse and Jean Héroard, Louis XIII's doctor, persuaded the king and Richelieu to consecrate the area "to the cultivation of medicinal plants, which your people might turn to in their infirmities, where the disciples of medicine might learn, and where those who teach it might address their needs." Five years of intensive work followed, supervised by de la Brosse, who also collaborated in the creation of the Luxembourg Gardens.

The results were hugely successful and even English visitors found it exceptional. From its inception, the handsome, useful, universal Jardin des Plantes was, indeed, the complete garden described by a seventeenth-century

English traveler, John Evelyn: "It is a large enclosure with all the varieties of terrain needed for the cultivation of medicinal plants. Its placement was well chosen, for it contains mounds, valleys, meadows, woods, and it is richly supplied with exotic plants. In the middle of the parterre there is a beautiful fountain. Adjoining this garden there is a beautiful house, a chapel, a laboratory, an orangery and everything needed by its director, who is still one of the king's first physicians."

When Jean Robin died, his son Vespasien continued his work: the first greenhouse was built and the large fountain basin was dug. He published catalogues such as *Hortius Regius*, and, above all, Vespasien Robin founded a

The "Gloriette de Buffon," the oldest metal structure in Paris, dominates the Jardin des Plantes (above). The Judas tree, spectacular in springtime with its bright pink blossoms, provides shade for the children's play area (facing). In May, the alpine garden, at the heart of the Jardin des Plantes, forms a mosaic of colors with Japanese pink primroses, Oriental red poppies and Caucasian catmint (following page).

botanical school, which was run by one of the royal doctors. Colbert, head of the royal administration, institutionalized the management of the garden and, in an excess of Puritanism, had the vines from which the administrators made their wine uprooted. The garden had a succession of illustrious administrators: Brongniart, Cassini, Geoffroy and the botanist and explorer Joseph Pitton de Tournefort. With the arrival of de Tournefort, the era of doctors came to an end, and they were replaced by naturalists and botanists: Lacépède, Jussieu, Lamarck, Adanson, Geoffroy Saint-Hilaire. Bernard de Jussieu had already planted his cedar (now in the alpine garden), and the male pistachio tree, through which Sébastien Vaillant was to discover the sexuality of plants, had already borne its fruits. In 1739 Comte de Buffon was appointed intendant of the garden with Jean Thouin as head gardener. The ambitions of the count, elected to the Science Academy at the young age of twenty-six, were immense. Assisted by Daubenton, he enlarged the garden, at the same time working on his vast *Histoire naturelle*. Buffon reigned over this domain while Daubenton, promoted to researcher, "would shut himself away in the Cabinet for days on end," according to Cuvier, in order to classify the existing collections.

On August 20, 1790, the National Assembly requested a group of petitioning "officers" of the garden including Daubenton, Lacépède, Lamarck, Thouin and Brongniart to hold a deliberative assembly. In the course of two sittings they decided on the name of the garden, the Muséum d'Histoire Naturelle, defined the strictly "scientific" aims of the institution, laid down its rules and determined the salaries. There was a short period during which Bernardin de Saint-Pierre sat as the honorable successor to Buffon. Daubenton then took over and was able to fulfill the dream of the author of *Paul et Virginie*: the creation of a menagerie. It was made possible by the wholesale requisitioning of animals from the fairgrounds of Paris and the royal menageries, coupled with the enthusiasm of the young Geoffroy Saint-Hilaire. This menagerie soon became so popular that the arrival of a giraffe was heralded as a national event; a medal struck for the occasion bears the inscription: "On June 30, 1827, Her Highness the Giraffe made her entrance into Paris."

Although open to everyone, the superbly beautiful Jardin des Plantes is nevertheless a laboratory-garden, in the eighteenth-century meaning of the word, or even an "academy," according to seventeenth-century usage.

With two and a half million visitors a year, the Jardin des Plantes is the fourth largest tourist attraction in Paris. It represents one of the most powerful utopias that man has ever dreamed of: to master all the forms of Nature and to gather them together in a single spot. As a marvelous collection of plants and animals, the Jardin des Plantes is a microcosm that is both seductive and terrifying. The world is revealed as either angelic, through the judiciously planted and colorful areas of trees and flowers peopled with languid animals; or diabolic, inhabited by strange trees, or carnivorous

Under these majestic glass roofs proliferate the most surprising species in the Jardin des Plantes: Mexican peyote and Hottentot fig trees, bamboos and Tonkin vines.

shaped shadows. From here, the garden presents its most imposing and rigorous appearance, though the view is cut short by the zoological building. The gardens slope gently upward and the walks, planted with a double row of square-cut plane trees, enhance the French-style vista. The parterres to the right are composed of four *carrés*, or squares: Carré Mirbel, Carré Thouin, Carré des Rosiers and Carré Ducaisne. Each one has lawns and plants; close to one hundred varieties of begonias, pinks, geraniums, heliotropes, dahlias and cannas form superb beds, in which red is the prominent color, followed closely by yellow and purple.

From mid-May to the end of June, the Iris Garden, between the paleontological and cryptogamic galleries, is a riot of nearly four hundred varieties of irises; it is bordered by two ancient mulberry trees with gnarled trunks supported by braces, and a collection of clematis was planted next to it in 1989. In the courtyard of the paleontological laboratory, a male ginkgo tree has been grafted with a female branch whose fruit, which look like pretty mirabelle plums, ripen in the autumn.

plants, Harlequin-like chameleons, giant spiders, phantoms and dioramas of equatorial animals.

The garden is an immense "curiosity cabinet" where knowledgeable visitors lean closely to read the labels — written meticulously in French or Latin — as if to verify, with a certain satisfaction, what he already knows.

On the Seine side, from the Carré Brongniart, the garden opens out into a vast parterre divided by the main walkway and the *allées* Cuvier and Buffon. The picnic area is edged with Judas trees, the oldest of which were planted by Buffon around 1785. A sorb tree and a black cypress cast generous, strangely

The menagerie, a major attraction in the nineteenth century, includes a lion house, a monkey house, a large aviary, a snake house and a bear pit. Nearby stand the sugar maple and the old Corsican black pine planted by Antoine-Laurent de Jussieu between 1774 and 1784.

The marvels of the alpine garden follow: 2,000 plants brought from the Caucasus, Corsica, Morocco, the Alps and the Himalayas grow in close proximity to each other thanks to careful planting, the shade of the trees and the types of soil, siliceous or chalky. Next there is a playground by a pond and a pleasant lawn with a bilobate ginkgo that is some 150 years

About 200 varieties of dahlias bloom in the Jardin des Plantes in August. Dwarf and giant dahlias form superbly colored alleys.

old. In the autumn the yellowing leaves make it look like a gigantic nugget of gold.

Facing a Cretan maple with a million glittering leaves lies the Grand Labyrinthe, known as "Buffon's Labyrinth." A stairway bordered with yew, evergreen oak, maple and box trees leads to the top of the former Butte Coypeau where some of the old Oriental thujas still stand.

The terrace of the kiosk or "Buffon's summer house"— the oldest metal structure in Paris (1788 and restored in 1984) — offers an unexpected view of the city and of the garden itself. Marie Antoinette visited Buffon here; Madame Roland used to meet the naturalist Bosc; and Chateaubriand, Hortense Allart.

The escarpment, the *fabriques* and the rare perfumes in this part of the garden make it a sort of haven of English and Romantic styles: *Horas non numero nisi serenas* ("I count only the cloudless hours") is engraved on the armillary sphere of the kiosk. The hothouses, bombed in 1871, have been restored to their former glory. The square Australian hothouse contains Mediterranean and Australian plants, while the Mexican one houses superb cactuses and euphorbia. The "Grande Serre" or Winter Garden, an extension of the Mexican hothouse built in 1937, includes an astonishing variety of tropical plants.

Businessmen with attaché cases cross the garden diagonally from east to west as a shortcut from Austerlitz station to the Latin Quarter. Students from Censier cross its southern corner to reach Jussieu. The boy with his donkey cart disappeared in the sixties but, at all hours of the day, in every season, the walk that crosses from Buffon to Cuvier is still packed with children who cling to the fence with both hands as they carry on strange and fascinating conversations with the zoo animals. The parents hurry through, but Rainer Maria Rilke's tiger — he wrote this poem here at the end of 1902 — still fills childish heads: "His sight exhausted by staring at the numberless bars / he can no longer take anything in / For her, it is as if there were thousands of bars / and no life behind those thousands of bars. . . ."

Besides being a teaching garden, the Jardin des Plantes is also a place to relax. At dawn and sundown it is filled with joggers. Peaceful retirees meet regularly in the allée des Dames, named for the games of checkers played there; the elderly come to sit on the old metal chairs, and some days there are as many as twenty-four games of chess in progress, sometimes played under the shelter of the

Through the humid atmosphere of the Jardin des Plantes greenhouse stretches the luxuriant jungle, with a stunning exuberance of palm and banana trees, ficus and cycas, giant ferns and Indian fig.

Hothouses of the Jardin des Plantes) and *Femme se promenant dans un jardin exotique* (Woman Strolling in an Exotic Garden). All of Rousseau's canvases contain the familiar dream of his period: a return to nature and exoticism.

This Eden-like view of nature is found again in the warm colors of Raoul Dufy's pair of decorative panels, *Les Explorateurs* and *Les Naturalistes* that ornament the walls of the library.

A garden of crystals, plants, animals and anthropology: the Jardin des Plantes, glittering under a brilliant sun, is the poetic home par excellence of science and modern man. In this sense it is a perpetual work of art.

porch roof of the ancient anatomy gallery. The card players sit opposite, on the edge of a small field with a pretty stream in which the geese and ducks hide their nests. On the rue de Cuvier side, quiet games of checkers are in progress and, when the sun is at its zenith, the players move to the shelter of a handsome apricot tree now that the once-great elms, cut down, no longer provide a quiet, shady refuge.

Above all, with it sumptuous world of plants, rare flowers, exotic trees, flaming graminaceae and even weeds, this garden has always seemed to be an earthly paradise. During the Revolution, the enlargement of the menagerie made it a Noah's Ark. Painters came to sketch the animals: Gustave Moreau, Antoine-Louis Barye and Eugène Delacroix were drawn to the lions and their violence; Rosa Bonheur saw the animals as tame, trusting and gentle; Honoré Daumier preferred to draw the public gawking at the bears, monkeys and elephants. Contemporary artists still go to the Jardin des Plantes: Monory, Ernest Pignon-Ernest, Olivier O. Olivier and Gilles Aillaud.

Douanier Rousseau, a regular visitor to the park at the turn of the century, created a naive vision of Eden with *Parisienne dans les serres du Jardin des plantes* (Parisian in the

The orchard in the Luxembourg Gardens is a compendium of forms: the oblique, twisted or candelabra-shaped "cordons" form works of art (top).
It is not unusual to meet people wearing strange hats in the Luxembourg Gardens: they are learning about bees in the recently restored apiary (above). The Luxembourg orchard, the only one of its kind in Paris, produces two tons of fruit each year (raspberries, figs, persimmons, blackcurrants) and includes some very old varieties (facing).

*Many varieties of apple compete with the
pears in the Luxembourg orchard (above). As soon as
the fruit forms it is wrapped to
protect it from worms; pesticides are not used (facing).*

The Jardin d'Acclimatation in Boulogne, the hothouses in Auteuil, the garden of the École du Breuil, the zoo and the Parc de Vincennes are also enchanting teaching gardens.

Not far from the Bois de Vincennes, the sixty-one magnificent greenhouses in Auteuil also form a botanical garden. Placed within a French-style garden, every tree, bush, plant and flower is labeled. It is open to the public all year and hosts exhibitions and fairs, as well as concerts in the greenhouses, where the acoustics are excellent. Some two and a half million species (six hundred varieties of orchids and collections of begonias, azaleas, chrysanthemums and even carnivorous plants) are grown in this municipal flower garden.

The zoo at Vincennes is just one of the many attractions of the forest, which include footpaths (twenty-six kilometers); cycle paths (nine kilometers); bridle paths (nineteen kilometers); and the play areas of the Belle Étoile, Saint Hubert, the École du Breuil and the Parc Floral.

The garden of the du Breuil municipal horticultural and arboricultural school — created at the end of the last century in order to train gardeners for the Parisian parks, gardens and squares and transferred to the Bois de Vincennes in 1936 — is itself a botanical paradise. The collection of plants, labeled and classified, is found in the flowering beds in the main courtyard and the landscape garden, the arboretum, the orchard, the tropical hothouses and the rose garden.

An old cloister garden, the Babylone Garden preserved its orchard and its charming alleys bordered by apple trees growing in "cordons" (above). In the teaching garden of the École de Pharmacie, a secret garden near Luxembourg, the greenhouses are already one hundred years old (facing).

*The greenhouses at the École de Pharmacie contain
medical, nutritional and Mediterranean plants destined for the students'
work and research laboratories. Part of the garden is reserved for
toxic plants like lilies-of-the-valley. Homeopathic plants and scented
plants are cultivated in a basin (above).*

Most of the trees in the arboretum, which includes close to six hundred species organized according to family groups (and some rare trees such as ehretia, xanthocera and cunninghamia), were planted in the 1940s and 1950s. In the meticulously maintained landscape garden, there are collections of heathland plants and peonies surrounded by remarkable trees — chestnut, liquidambar, plane — and in and around the rockery grow alpine plants, Japanese maples and evergreen oaks. The perennials, grouped into decorative clumps, form mixed borders that alternate with varieties of hedges. The orchard is designed according to species (about three hundred) and shape (espalier-trained or standard). It is best visited in the autumn, for it contains mainly apple and pear trees. The rose garden has two hundred varieties of roses. The fruticetum contains five hundred varieties of bushes and climbing plants laid out in thematic beds. The tropical hothouses are full of marvelous plants, while the pond full of delightful waterlilies would have captivated Monet.

The Luxembourg orchards, descendants of the nursery of the old Chartreux Abbey, include over two hundred varieties of apple and pear trees trained against the wall to form rows and fan-shaped espaliers on wires. In the winter, the bare shapes, the result of years of frequent, expert and precise pruning, have a sparseness that is reminiscent of the severe strength of the century that produced them. But in spring, clumps of small pink and white flowers enhanced by the bright green of twigs and branches are evocative of the sweet disorder of medieval *orceads*; it becomes a seasonal symphony, a delightful feast, a marvelous sight.

Despite their attractions, playgrounds, concerts and exhibitions, modern Parisian gardens can no longer provide the vibrant pleasures of the great aristocratic gardens of the past.

Love, culture, initiation: since Eden, gardens have taught knowledge that cannot be put into words. During the Enlightenment, some follies existed not only for pleasure, but were used for Masonic rituals as dangerous as those suffered by Tamino and Pamina at the end of the Magic Flute. Nearer to our own time, and in a rather more prosaic way, Parisian adolescents used to discover in the squares and gardens the mysteries of love that could not be learned in class. Rival gangs gathered there to experience their first thrill of love, their first dates, and become, as Brassens said in one of his songs, "lovers who peck at each other on the public benches."

It is not surprising that children prefer the delights of less-controlled surroundings to the amusement parks, play areas or even adventure playgrounds that functionalist concerns have installed in Parisian public gardens; despite their sophisticated equipment, they are not very interesting. The slides are always a little too short, and the maze is explored too quickly. Except for the smallest of children, the end of the street, the back yards and apartment stairways are infinitely more fascinating.

Furthermore, modern Parisian gardens have become much too "public" for lovers to enjoy their secret pleasures there. Of course, Paris still has many rustic places in which love thrives. But even though childhood discoveries and adolescent initiation happen much more frequently outdoors than in the confined environment of school, the atmosphere that once reigned in Parisian gardens no longer exists.

The bandstands sometimes replay favorite old tunes, yet they do not evoke the same emotion.

These amazing gardens with hillocks, waterfalls, grottoes, arbors and woods brightly illuminated at night, and with bandstands where the first creators of Parisian songs would perform, are all gone. Gone, too, are most of the *fabriques* from the Trianon and the gardens of the cafés-concerts of the Moulin Rouge.

Far from the Astérix, Mirapolis and the soon to be opened EuroDisney amusement park on the outskirts of Paris, children are still fascinated by the newborn 200-kilo baby elephant in the Vincennes Zoo, while others clutch the three franc, twenty centimes fee and head for one of the ten little wooden horses of the merry-go-round managed by Madame Léone, a smiling little woman in the Parc Montsouris.

Two world wars and technical advances put an end to the open-air dance halls of the nineteenth century such as the Bal des Tilleuls, the Closerie des Lilas, the summer Alcazar, the Jardin de Virginie and the Château des Fleurs.

Small terra-cotta pots are used by the gardeners at the Auteuil greenhouses to repot flowers and plants (top). Many different species are grown (above). Charming and wild, the orchids in the Auteuil greenhouses captivate the visitor who, amazed, will discover more than 600 species and varieties (facing).

The Auteuil greenhouses use modern techniques such as
automatic ventilation, misting and double-glazed windows (above).
Behind the drops of dew, the flowers may be admired, although they are
not fully revealed (above). Two sumptuous date palms from Madagascar
blossom beneath the central dome of the palmarium at
Auteuil (facing). On the smooth waters of the lake, the boat crosses the
Bois de Boulogne in the changing light (following page).

5

CITY SQUARES
AND WOODS

This scene could have taken place on a summer's night in 1924. The cynical seducer may have been Marcel Noll; or perhaps André Breton, who yearned for the forbidden garden; or even the poet Louis Aragon, in the guise of Le Paysan de Paris. Who it was is of little importance. But Buttes-Chaumont has never seemed quite the same since Aragon wrote this tale: "All that is strange about man, all that belongs to the vagabond, to the lost soul in him, can be expressed in these two syllables: garden."

The magic began with the name given to this 61-acre park (that with the 79-acre Jardin des Plantes is one of the two largest gardens inside Paris) when it was opened in 1867: the Buttes-Chaumont. Aragon described it as "a mirage with all that is inherently tangible in it . . . a great oasis in a popular district . . . an unsavory area redolent of murder . . . a crazy place, born from the bosom of an architect struggling with the conflict between Jean-Jacques Rousseau's ideas and the reality of living conditions in Paris," and even "Mesopotamia."

Yet the Buttes-Chaumont had always been a dismal place, the exact opposite of a garden. The word Chaumont comes from *calvus mons* (bald mountain) and, although it may be an exaggeration to evoke Moussorgsky's black sabbath, nevertheless the macabre Montfaucon gibbet was nearby, in what is now the Place du Colonel-Fabien. In those days the Buttes lay at the edge of Paris; it was nothing more than a sinister gypsum quarry. There were no trees or greenery to relieve the unattractive site. It was next transformed into a dumping ground when Baron Haussmann turned Paris into a vast construction site. It required an incredible feat of imagination to transform this cesspool into a paradise on earth, even though the project had the blessing of both Napoleon III and the baron, who wanted the park to provide recreation for the poorer people living on the east side of Paris.

And yet a paradise is exactly what engineer Alphand and gardener Barillet-Deschamps proposed to create. They were even quite daring, despite the short amount of time available before Napoleon was to officially inaugurate the garden on the occasion of the 1867 Universal Exposition. Rather than attempting to camouflage the tormented nature of the site, they decided to enhance it instead, and thus achieve a maximum of unusual effects.

The streets and the railway that cross the park were therefore included in its layout and

The Belvedere at Buttes-Chaumont has been cleaned and restored to its original brilliance (above). A forest of pine trees, peaceful in the tormented landscape of Buttes-Chaumont (facing).

became an attractive component of the entire design. This was undoubtedly done for economic reasons, but there was also a deliberate artistic intent to emphasize the urban character of the park and to make it an integral element of the city's network. The designers did not wish to exclude the city from the park; they realized that open spaces were essential to the hygiene of the growing metropolis. According to Alphand, visitors can enjoy "the sight of a station, a factory or any such building as long as it is set in a proper landscape." Applying the techniques of the royal German gardener, Prince Pückler-Muskau, a friend and correspondent of Napoleon III for whom "anything of interest that lies far away should, in a manner of speaking, be drawn into our domain in such a way

as to disguise its boundaries," Barrillet-Deschamps drew the city into the park through optical effects and transformed it into a setting for, and an integral part of, his rustic design.

When the gardeners replanted the circumference of the grottoes at Buttes-Chaumont, they were suspended in space like climbers beneath the astonished eyes of the public (top). The landscape of the rock gardens of the park, where the Crève-Coeur streams meet (above). The hanging bridges above the crevasses, cliffs and waterfalls (facing). The trees at Buttes-Chaumont are home to the titmouse, warbler, siskin and the song thrush (following page).

The gashes left by the former quarry were accentuated and made to resemble a Jurassic combe, or ravine. A lush landscape with mountain plateaus, fields, brooks and huge trees planted in groves and glades is pierced by a sheer cliff-like promontory that stops abruptly to reveal a lake set in the valley below.

The real genius of Barillet and his engineer J. Darcel, however, is revealed in the great Belevédère rock; this hill is not merely a decoration, however surprising and spectacular it may be. The interwoven climbing paths lead to the marvelous elements flanking the hill: a delightful little terrace lined with benches; a giddying footbridge; a grotto farther on; an inviting flat spot on the

rock that, bathed in sunshine, is a perfect place to rest; and even a "temple" copied from the Temple of the Sybils at Tivoli, perched at the top of the cliff.

Wandering through the park after sundown, as in Louis Aragon's *Le Paysan de Paris*, is a truly surrealist experience: "A white ghost stands on a stone abutment like a diver on his board, the ivy climbs vertiginously toward it as he looms, a total void between his legs, on the great arch below that leads to the sloping field in front of the Belvédère, kneeling on a black coffee cup. André Breton then exclaims, 'Look, you can see the bridge from here, the famous Bridge of Suicides. . . .'" As these modern explorers of the bizarre penetrate farther into the park, they seem to be walking through the illustrations of the Hetzel edition of Jules Verne's *Les Indes noires, L'Île mystérieuse* or *Voyage au centre de la terre*. Aragon continues, " . . . And there are also the snaking paths, the lake with its sleeping birds, Mandarin ducks at which we throw stones, though, knowing we'll never hit them, they stay put on their perches in the water, unmoved. . . . Behold the department of dreams: through a crevice in the artificial rock, a passageway to the bottom of a dale with a running brook hastening — waterfall ahead — to its doom . . ."

The Buttes-Chaumont, a horticultural masterpiece of the Second Empire, forms part of the series of open spaces that punctuate the stone-clad city as redesigned by Baron Haussmann. "It took us a long time to accept what he did, but today he has been vindicated; public gardens are an essential part of any city," Alphand noted in 1867. Shortly after he began his major book, *Les Promenades de Paris*, in which he developed a system for the design of public spaces, treating them as part of a whole that includes roadside borders, areas of trees,

The small waterfall at Buttes-Chaumont crosses the "pine tree knoll" where, strangely, coniferous trees are no longer to be seen.

*At Buttes-Chaumont, standing proudly in
the middle of the path, two chestnut trees in the form of a candelabra
have just celebrated their 125th birthday (top).
At the first sign of cold weather, the park becomes a refuge for seagulls
whose cries stifle the songs of every other bird (above).*

therefore ought to consider installing large public gardens at cardinal points inside its walls. The need for this is obvious as one watches those beautiful gardens, which used to attract such huge crowds on public holidays, disappear one by one."

This alarming statement alerted Napoleon III, who believed in a "democratic imperialism" along the lines of Saint-Simon's economic doctrines. Following the coup d'etat of December 2, 1851 that made him emperor, he implemented a policy of law and order that established the power of industry alongside that of the state, and supported public ownership coupled with a strong and repressive administration. While exiled in England, he had admired the public parks and private gardens of London's West End and their air of wealth and sobriety that reflected the vigor of the British Empire. As soon as he came to power, he personally addressed the problem of the shortage of gardens in Paris, beginning with the Bois de Boulogne.

This first attempt, however, nearly ended in disaster. The landscape-gardener Varé and the architect Hittorf, to whom Napoleon III had entrusted the project, were unable to overcome the enormous difficulties of road planning and hydraulics. On his appointment as prefect of

Paris in 1855, Haussmann took advantage of their failure to impose his personal choice: engineer Adolphe Alphand, whom he placed at the head of a specially created Promenades et Plantations department. He also appointed Jean-Pierre Barillet, known as Barillet-Deschamps, and the architect Davioud as assistants.

Napoleon III, Haussmann, Alphand, Barillet-Deschamps, Davioud: a bourgeoisie that detested the likes of Nerval, Hugo and Baudelaire could not have chosen a better team to destroy, in the name of hygiene and comfort, the Paris that these poets loved. The emperor's role was minimal; he was never more than a financial backer and sleeping partner. Haussmann's contribution — regardless of the effect his "military" lines had on the architecture of medieval Paris — was an overall vision of the project and a capacity for training and managing an exceptionally competent team. Despite the somewhat bucolic title of his department (which sent his Polytechnic colleagues into fits of uncontrollable laughter), Alphand was clever enough to realize that promenades and plantations could also include streets, and therefore, urban development in general. For his part, Davioud distinguished himself by inventing a new style of architecture, a subdued blending of eclectic exoticism that culminated at the Universal Exposition of 1875, when he crowned the hill of the Trocadéro with a gigantic half-Moorish, half-Russian *fabrique*. As for Barillet-Deschamps, he was elbowed aside by his masters, who shamelessly attributed his talent to themselves. Yet he was a great artist, considered by his pupils to be on a par with Le Nôtre. His reputation was so well established that, after landscaping the Buttes-Chaumont and some marvelous temporary gardens for the 1875 Exposition, he was summoned to Vienna to redesign the Prater. At the request of the

The magnificent arched bridge offers one of the most romantic views of Buttes-Chaumont (above). Among the pine trees, strollers enjoy the lawns (facing).

Sublime Porte, he later traveled to Cairo and Constantinople, where he designed several parks and gardens before his death in 1871.

How did Barillet-Deschamps, who came from such humble origins, manage to meet such highly placed people?

It was in Bordeaux that Haussmann, newly embarked on a career in administration, first noticed the unusual authority of the young highways engineer, Adolphe Alphand. When Haussmann returned to the capital of Aquitaine as head of the Gironde prefecture, he was given the opportunity to entertain the new Prince-President whom, as a member of the Ordre political party, he had vigorously supported. The young prefect set about organizing a special reception. But to whom could he turn in that austere town? This is where Alphand came in: his incisive mind, talent for organization and mastery of engineering techniques resulted in a spectacular party that Louis-Napoleon was to remember with such pleasure that, after the Empire was reestablished, one of his first decisions was to summon Haussmann to Paris. Meanwhile, Alphand had particularly appreciated the work of a horticulturalist whose knowledge of plants and design of flower beds had produced some sumptuous borders. The son of a farmer from the Tours area, he kept shop in Bordeaux under the name of Barillet-Deschamps. He had been discovered by the philanthropist Demetz who, in order to complete the young man's training, had placed him with Gustave Thouin, head gardener at the Muséum.

Gustave Thouin was the son of the great André Thouin, explorer and principal gardener of the Jardin des Plantes. Expanding on his father's work, he published an astonishing anthology, *Plans raisonnés de toutes les espèces de jardins* (Description Plans of All Types of Gardens, 1820), which served as the basis — along with Repton's and, later, Pückler-Muskau's work — for a new style in parks that adapted them to their public vocation, known as the "landscapist" style. The enterprising Bülher brothers had helped to spread it to a great many provincial towns, although with uneven results; one of the more spectacular successes is the Parc de la Tête-d'Or in Lyon.

Thus, despite his peasant background, Barillet-Deschamps was far from being a self-taught landscape-gardener, unlike many of the flower sellers who called themselves horticulturalists. The only work he ever published was about pansies, of all things, in which the preface, dedicated to one of his Viennese colleagues, touched delicately on the transfer of pollen by means of a paintbrush. However, Barillet was undoubtedly the designer of the "promenades" of the Second Empire, even though Alphand later wrote that he himself produced the work (he even neglected to mention Barillet's name in his book). Haussmann confirmed Barillet's contribution in his memoirs, recounting that, while the guest of Ismaïl Pasha in Constantinople in 1873, he came across a landscape he was "acquainted with." In other words, he recognized the style of his ex-gardener Barillet-Deschamps. After praising its "great qualities," such as "a perfect understanding of the distribution of the ground between undulating lawns, groves of trees or rare bushes, baskets of plants and flowers," he turned on its creator and criticized "a certain abuse of details and too few *allées*." He then added, proving that it was indeed Barillet and not Alphand who produced the drawings of new promenades in the days when he, Haussmann, was in charge of the reconstruction of Paris: "I wanted, in embracing all of the park, . . . to give more breadth to the parts unfortunately cut by useless paths."

The swan at Buttes-Chaumont carries his solitude around with him on the waters of the lake. He has just lost his companion, and remains indifferent to the noisy friendship of the ducks.

"Useless paths," "an abuse of detail." Fortunately, many of these so-called "defects" exist today in the Buttes-Chaumont and in the Bois de Boulogne and Bois de Vincennes.

The Bois de Boulogne, set in the old Rouvray forest, was designed by Napoleon III for the inhabitants of the fashionable districts of Paris. Even if now some of its paths shelter a dubious kind of fauna, ranging from whores to transvestites and voyeurs, the grandeur of its facilities is impressive: there is Longchamp, a horsetrack for flat and obstacle racing; the Roland-Garros tennis courts; the Pré Catelan, for luxurious entertainment; the Shakespeare garden with its theater of greenery; and the Paris Polo Club.

The Bois de Boulogne offers an astonishing variety of landscapes, all contained in a relatively small area: two lakes on different levels (Varé's mistake, which Alphand corrected by creating superb waterfalls), grottoes, kiosks, pavilions, chalets, bridges, "gates" (now reduced to a few remains), lawns and romantic trees, an amusement park, and the marvelous Bagatelle.

As soon as it was opened, "le Bois" became the most frequented spot in Paris, and its *allées* became, in the words of Baudelaire, "long avenues of high life." And however strong Baudelaire's aversion to Haussmann's "hygienist" pretensions, the author of *Tableaux Parisiens* was not one to spurn such a meeting place of fashion and elegant dalliance. In an article, "Le Peintre de la vie moderne" ("The Painter of Modern Life"), published in *Le Figaro* at the end of 1863,

Beneath the branches of a large tree, the wonderful diaphanous light of early morning on the lake at the Bois de Boulogne (above). The calmness of the Boulogne lake is deceptive. In the water's depths, the pike sows terror among the carps, roaches and gudgeons (facing).

*A romantic boat ride on the lower lake
in the Bois de Boulogne to reach the Chalet de l'Île, a popular restaurant
in summer (top). A boat trip on the lake amid the comical
ducks is one of the great bucolic pleasures of the Bois de Boulogne (above).
The leaves collected in autumn nourish
the humus of the flower beds and the undergrowth (facing).*

Baudelaire wrote: "Sometimes there are wayside stops — camps, one might call them — with dozens of carriages, where slender young men and women decked in the eccentric garb the seasons allow, hoist themselves up onto cushions, seats or tops of carriages, to watch some turfing event flying by in the distance. . . . The carriage sets off at a spanking pace along a drive striped with alternate shadow and light, bearing off an indolent beauty reclining as if in an easy chair, faintly acknowledging the compliments whispered in her ear and lazily abandoning herself to the breeze of the drive." And if, contrary to Zola's evocation of this haunt of luxury, display and leisure where "in the heavy summer afternoons . . . high above the horizon, the sun filled the hollow leaves with melted golden light, set fire to the high branches and

transformed this sea of leaves into a sea of light," Baudelaire does not actually name the Bois de Boulogne, there can be no doubt that he had it in mind when he was describing the watercolors of Constantin Guys, a great lover

When the sun sets, the wood returns to its wild state.
Then the song thrush with its sonorous refrain can be heard (top).
In the fall, the fires lit to clear the Bois de Boulogne
of its dead branches fill the park with ash-tinged mists and a
pungent smell (below).

of "le Bois": "At the end of the park, the woods grow green or russet, powdery or dark, according to the season or the time of day. Their recesses are filled with autumn mists, blue shadows, yellow rays, pink effulgence and slender lightning flashes that slice through the darkness like the stroke of a sword."

Perhaps the young Proust was thinking of Baudelaire when he went to the Bois to admire the outfits of the lovely Odette Swann. Yet several decades later, it was a man bruised by the defection of Madame de Stermaria who dragged Albertine along in the traces of the young aesthete he had once been. This time, however, no pleasures or gaiety remained. Time had done its sinister work, spoiling beauty and carefree youth: "We took a few steps forward under the greenish, almost

submarine, grotto formed by a thick grove, we could hear the wind unfurling and the rain spraying on its domed roof. I crushed dead leaves underfoot that bit into the earth like shells, and pushed aside chestnuts, as prickly as sea urchins, with my stick" (*Le Côté de Guermantes*, 1920).

The one-time haunt of snobs and elegant women is not quite what it used to be, and, although it retains the flavor of its aristocratic beginnings because of its proximity to Passy and Neuilly, the passing of time and advancing democracy have brought it closer in spirit to the Bois de Vincennes.

In Vincennes, no ghosts of "ladies of quality" haunt the banks of the de Gravelle or Daumesnil lakes, nor have they ever, even

Forest, maritime, Himalayan and Vancouver pines coexist in perfect harmony in the pine forest at the Bois de Boulogne (above). The quiet banks and wild horizon of the lake in the Bois de Vincennes carries the imagination far away from Paris (following page).

in literature. In a gesture that was deemed highly commendable and democratic at the time, the Bois de Vincennes was presented to "the workers of the eleventh and twelfth arrondissements" by Napoleon III in 1852. As they had done with the Bois de Boulogne, Alphand, Barillet-Deschamps and Davioud set about creating a picturesque environment threaded with drives, *allées* and paths. Lawns, flower beds, woods and high-standing groves were planted around several artificial lakes (des Minimes, Daumesnil, de Gravelle, de Saint-Mandé), complete with islands full of grottoes, pavilions and restaurants.

It was an instant success. Workers, seamstresses and ruffians were soon to be seen picnicking on the grass on Sunday afternoons in an atmosphere reminiscent of Renoir or

Casque d'Or. The addition of a zoo increased the park's popularity, and families still enjoy its many attractions: a hollow rock inhabited by a colony of baboons or macaques; a lion house; the famous pond around which

*Recently restored, the Rotunda, also called the
Temple of Love, can be seen above the Daumesnil Lake in the
Bois de Vincennes (top). Beneath the rotunda
lies the grotto of Reuilly Island, where even the waterfall scarcely
disturbs the silence (bottom).*

children cluster at five o'clock to watch the feeding of the fat seals; another pool by the paddocks full of trotting-horses.

The eastern edge of the park offers other distractions: bicycling, running, boating, bowls or football, the Parc Floral, the reconstructed old-style farmhouse, dancing in the lakeside *guinguettes*, or dance halls. Perhaps Vincennes, despite the medieval fortress that once served as a prison for Latude, Diderot, Mirabeau and the Marquis de Sade, has retained something of the solemnity of the oak under which, according to Froissard, Saint-Louis dispensed justice. Or perhaps the memory of the Colonial Exhibition held there in 1931, now in the nearby African and Oceanic Art Museum, still lingers in the foliage, the echo of a time when France fondly believed she was the alma mater of what she imagined were childlike peoples.

The amusement park of the Foire du Trône, the merry-go-rounds, the great ferris wheel: there is no end to the reminders of the Bois de Vincennes' proletarian past. The Paris celebrated in the songs of Francis Lemarque or Yves Montand, and that of Parisians who so enjoyed the Grands Boulevards and Luna-Park, offered a pastoral refuge at the Lac des Minimes. This Paris no longer exists; it is now the suburban dwellers who fill the woods with their holiday laughter, while the well-heeled inhabitants of the towns of Vincennes and Saint-Mandé indulge in more discreet pleasures.

The horticultural achievements of Haussmann, Alphand, Davioud and Barillet-Deschamps

The silhouette of a weeping sophora at Vincennes, as gnarled as those at Bagatelle.

maple and chestnut trees line the boulevards. A wide avenue such as boulevard Richard-Lenoir, covering close to two kilometers of the Saint-Martin canal, offers a succession of flower beds. Farther north, the canal reappears at the Square Frédéric Lemaître. This shady little area that, with Square Récollets, runs along several locks of the canal, was created after the Haussmann era in 1891, but it retains the same spirit. As opposed to the "open promenade" concept of the Champs-Élysées or boulevard Richard Lenoir, this landscaped garden was designed to fit into whatever "void" Baron Haussmann's reworking of Paris left unfilled.

were not, however, limited to these or other showpieces, such as the Buttes-Chaumont, the Bois, Parc Montsouris and the questionable transformations of Monceau and the Luxembourg Gardens (happily Alphand's plan to transform the Tuileries lock, stock and barrel into a landscaped park was never carried out). The team was also responsible for more modest projects: they planted trees and flowers along the avenues and boulevards, and in the malls and squares of the city.

On the west side of Paris, the avenue of the Empress, now avenue Foch, and, above all, the Champs-Élysées, have superb gardens that serve as settings for luxurious restaurants. In the spring, the terraces are transformed into immense parterres full of petunias, geraniums and dwarf dahlias planted in mosaic patterns, bordered by "Napoleon III-style" beds of evergreen shrubs (yew, aucuba, spindle trees, box, laurel, viburnum) that adorn the intersections. The side-lanes are separated from the main road by rows of horse chestnut, black pine, elm, magnolia, honey locust, hickory and mulberry trees.

In the more working-class districts, the trees and plants along the streets are less elaborate, but still attractive. Elm, plane, lime, poplar, cedrela, sophora, paulownia, robinia, catalpa,

This principle produced the great variety found in Parisian squares. Some of them, with vast lawns, parterres, flower beds and handsome walks bordered with noble trees, are gardens of generous proportions. Others have little more than a sand pit, a few benches and a meager plot of greenery squeezed into a tiny space.

Although the word "square" is of English origin, Parisian squares differ from their London counterparts by their unorthodox shapes — caused by the layout of the surrounding streets and blocks of buildings — and by their public vocation.

The ponies that take children for rides in the Luxembourg, Tuileries, Champ-de-Mars or Ranelagh gardens each evening return to their domain in the fifteenth arrondissement (top). Square Récamier is a marvelous refuge for strollers in search of a shady corner of greenery (below).

*The Quai de Valmy, an alley of gray granite
cobblestones beneath the shadow of magnificent black poplars,
runs along the Canal Saint-Martin. A bit of
country in the heart of Paris, the canal offers fishermen clear waters
inhabited by trout, carp, pike and crayfish (above).
At sunset, the Place des Vosges is illuminated by the pink of the
surrounding houses (following page).*

The Place des Vosges is unique in that it was planned; it was not merely a space left over from a thoroughfare and in need of embellishment. At the end of the sixteenth century Henry IV decided to stop the haphazard medieval growth of the city by creating a rectangular square in the heart of the Marais, framed by symmetrical buildings constructed in a homogenous style. The vast proportions of the square (12,700 square meters) made it much larger than the Place de Grève, or the parvis in front of Notre-Dame. It was an incredible luxury for the period, and the empty space of the royal square meant that it could be used for the staging of processions, carousels, jousts and fairs. However, Richelieu's decision to erect an equestrian statue of Louis XIII in the middle of the square and surround it with lawns drastically restricted this kind of

event. The Place des Vosges then almost became a square in the English sense, for the inhabitants asked for box-edged beds which would have necessitated its privatization. After much negotiating, a compromise was reached. The garden was planted with geometric flower beds and stayed open to the public, although it was enclosed by railings. Alphand retained these when he redesigned the Place. Unfortunately, the vague classicism of his design is mediocre, or at least out of character. The cluttered aspect of the square, with its trees, railings, street lamps, fountains, the copy of the statue of Louis XIII — the original was melted down for cannons during the Revolution — and all the accoutrements of a typical Haussmann-style garden, run counter to the orginal concept and make this square hard to appreciate. The great sense of space afforded

It is enchanting to stroll through the
Square des Batignolles. A river leads from the pond to a waterfall that
drops between two huge rocks from Fontainebleau.

180

soon as the pickaxes of the demolition workers have transformed a whole district into a huge empty space bleached white with plaster dust, gardeners appear with barrows full of turf and compost; one of them brings trees and rocks, another digs a pond, a third lays out walks edged with pots of flowers sunk into the ground and, eight days later, a narrow garden that has sprouted as if by magic is presented to the rambler."

The miracle of these urban gardens, which in the space of a few days rise up to fill the empty spaces of a city that is being constantly redrawn, linger in one's memories like never-forgotten childhood fairy tales.

At the creak of a door in its cast-iron grate the world is transformed: joy or sadness overwhelms, depending on the season or the mood. The sandy avenue crunches underfoot; old ladies seated on benches under the trees, innocently busy with their knitting, become wicked fairies disguised as grandmothers. The unsuspecting park guard prefers to stare at a young woman reading the employment columns of a national newspaper. Has he even noticed that there are two children kissing in the shrubbery?

A famous grandmother who, after years spent dazzling Paris, retired to a huge country garden to write stories for the children that we all still are, described her view of the city: "It is a setting, no more, so make the best of it. But it is the most wonderful, the most delightful of settings."

This grandmother, George Sand, was absolutely right. There is perhaps nothing more delightful in the whole of Paris than the squares and the gorgeous parks. More than simply letting the city breathe, they offer nests of greenery that enclose an artificial universe where our fantasies and tranquil dreams of adventure crystallize into reality.

by the harmonious rhythm of the façades, roofs and arcades that surround the square is spoiled by this comfortable bourgeois bric-a-brac.

This kind of bric-a-brac, however, contributes to the perfection of the best of Alphand's squares: Temple (1857), l'Observatoire (1867), Boucicault (built in 1875 and redesigned in 1969), Montholon (1863), la Trinité (1865), Maurice-Gardette (1872), la Place d'Italie (1878), Violet (1876), Batignolles (1862), Edouard Vaillant (1879) and even Épinettes, although this last dates from 1893. An article by Zola published in *Le Figaro* on June 18, 1867, recounts the creation of these squares: "From time to time, Paris, blinded by the dust, throws up an islet of greenery in the gray ocean of its houses. As

L'allée des Cygnes (Swan Alley), a poetic island in the middle of the Seine, no longer shelters swans; in winter, black-headed seagulls and mallard ducks nest here (above). Ivy plants wrap themselves around the parapet and plunge into the Seine at the base of Notre Dame (facing). The magnificent balustrade in the Parc de Saint-Cloud overlooks Paris (following page).

6

GARDEN ORNAMENTS

Every garden is a reflection of our distant past that emerges with the Eden-like candor of childhood. Wherever man creates them, they retain a little of their "earthiness" amid art and science. By definition a garden is traversed by wide or narrow, straight or curving paths, and the ground between is planted with grass, shrubs, trees and flowers. The open spaces are dotted with pagodas, merry-go-rounds, kiosks, fountains and statues. Urban gardens, whenever they are created, are linked to a cosmogonic ideal — one that may be subtle or stereotyped — that is reflected in the individual design. In this sense follies, like Tschumi's red erector-set shapes or Buren's columns, are as much a part of Parisian gardens as Buffon's green labyrinth in the Jardin des Plantes or the statues in the Tuileries.

The descriptions of the first Tuileries Gardens, created for Catherine de' Medici in the sixteenth century, reveal the marvelous baroque inspiration of the design: the walls inside the Palissy grottoes were covered in colored stoneware snakes, lizards, birds and vegetables; water tumbled from a terrace over baked earth rocks into a pond filled with stoneware fish.

The classicism of the gardens at Saint-Cloud, Sceaux, the Tuileries and the Palais-Royal cannot be ascribed to their layout alone: these gardens were the product of an overall concept in which fountains, woods (now destroyed) and statues were signs and symbols creatively placed alongside the vegetation to achieve a remarkable completeness.

That gardens should be "lands of illusion," as Carmontelle stated in *Jardin de Monceau près de Paris* (1799), is obvious. Of all the Parisian parks, Monceau, in fact, was treated with the greatest imagination; here a mass of

cosmopolitan *fabriques* was assembled into a studied cultural disorder. An enchanted stream ran through a magic forest filled with servants dressed as Tartars or turbaned Hindus, leading animals from Africa and Asia. Through this accumulation of effects and curios, Carmontelle was extolling the use of imagination and even the theatricalization of nature. Hegel, in *Aesthetics*, described French gardens as "a nature that is thus transformed into a vast abode open to the skies," and he defined the art of gardening as "applying oneself to the transformation of the natural landscape, treating it as architecture in order to make it harmonize with real buildings."

The French nineteenth-century picturesque style differed from the eighteenth-century

The Stag, sculpted by Le Duc in 1885, is one of the most powerful works in the Luxembourg Gardens (above). The statues in the Tuileries are a regular attraction for the children, who are unimpressed by the great age of these stones (facing).

nostalgia for ivy-clad broken columns and ruins in that it used romantic components such as ravines and cliffs taken from nature itself, and drew heavily on exotic and colonial sources.

Today, at long last, Parisian gardens are no longer designed in opposition to the city, as mere patches of countryside that provide fresh air, according to the principles of a hygienist and anglophile Empire, but in conjunction with the city. They are cultural objects clearly marked by their modern, urban and technical environment.

Fountains existed early on in the first gardens of Paris-Lutetia. They were designed to provide water to thirsty citizens, which explains why they were usually situated

at intersections, in markets and on street corners; many of them exist to this day. They were also in cloister gardens, and medieval *orceads* were frequently planted around a decorated spring. Water was brought from Montmartre, Belleville and Ménilmontant by an ingenious Roman system: the water ran from an aqueduct into a reservoir that had holes along the side; these in turn were connected to conduits that led to privately owned water towers. It was not until the reign of Philippe Auguste that Parisian water became public property.

Although the Maubuée fountain, now on the corner of rue Saint-Martin and rue de Venise, is the oldest fountain in the capital, the fountain of the Innocents in the square of the same name is certainly the earliest designed

In the Luxembourg Gardens, the reflection of the vases in the water accentuates the Florentine atmosphere of the Medici fountain.

as an integral part of a square. It was constructed in the thirteenth century and rebuilt under Henry II, when Italian fashion introduced richly ornamented fountains into gardens. Bernini called it "the most beautiful object in France," even though it did not actually operate until 1892, when water was piped from the Ourcq canal. Frequently moved, this handsome loggia carved by Jean Goujon and Pierre Lescot became the centerpiece of the Square des Innocents through Davioud's intervention.

In the Luxembourg Gardens, the Medici fountain is no longer that built by Salomon de Brosse, Biart and Francine. It is no longer the main architectural ornament of the sixteenth-century royal gardens, nor the dazzling allegory of the pagan and the

Christian, that once-indispensable symbol of the "pleasure garden." Although Chalgrin preserved the fountain, Gisors, architect of the Luxembourg Gardens under the Second Empire, moved it to make way for his new basins. The wonderful *Leda* designed by Goujon was placed against the Medici fountain, and two prudish wood nymphs by Klagmann were added to it during the nineteenth century. However, the pleasantly shady aspect of the pond, bordered by cast-iron grillwork decorated with romantic shallow basins, gives this fountain sufficient calm, majesty and mystery to tempt the stroller to linger there still.

Past the legendary octagonal basin that lies in the middle of the gardens surrounded by flower beds, the fountain of the Four Corners

The masterful The Four Corners of the World *by Carpeaux, one of the prettiest fountains in Paris, in the Marco Polo Garden.*

of the World (from which Oceania is missing) leaps toward the Observatory on the other side of the park. Legrain created the sculptures of the signs of the Zodiac, and Frémiet the vigorous sea horses in this collective work supervised by Davioud. Above it rises Carpeaux's masterpiece in which young girls carry the globe through the sky. The overall effect is of blinding movement; the invitingly cool water splashes near the trees while, in the distance, at the Observatory, Time is symbolized by a metal bar. The Paris meridian lies nine minutes and twenty-one seconds ahead of Greenwich.

When the autumn light falls on the statue and students from the École Alsacienne, the Lycée Montaigne, the Faculty of Pharmacy and the Institute of Art and Archeology cross through the garden, this beautiful spot in Paris may be the loveliest sight in the world.

In Square Paul Langevin in the Latin Quarter, next to the remains of the ancient Philippe Auguste enclosure, some fragments of the fountain belonging to the Saint-Germain-des-Prés Abbey lean against the wall of the École Polytechnique, where they were placed when the boulevard was built. This fountain, also known as Childebert's fountain, once stood at the rue des Ciseaux entrance to the Abbey.

Not far away is the Square du Puits-de-l'Ermite, where a sixteenth-century tanner named Adam l'Hermite dug a well; from here there is a view of the the Paris mosque and its minaret.

The Jardin de l'Archevêché on the Île de la Cité, renamed Square Jean XXIII, was built on waste ground that was once rue de l'Abreuvoir. A neo-Gothic fountain containing a Virgin and Child and three archangels is set in a niche, but the garden's interest lies less in the fountain itself than in the view it affords of the apse and buttresses of Notre Dame.

The de la Paix fountain in the allée du Séminaire is one of fifteen fountains ordered by Napoleon I in 1806. Originally erected in the Place Saint-Sulpice, it was considered out of proportion to its environment and was replaced by the *Orateurs sacrés*. It was moved to the Marché Saint-Germain before coming to rest on the promenade of rue Bonaparte in 1835. The life of a small fountain in Paris is not a restful one!

Rome may be the city of nocturnal and dreamlike monumental fountains — so well depicted in Fellini's films — but Paris undoubtedly originated the great basins in which dazzling jets of water play in the light of day.

The fountain in the Luxembourg Gardens is remarkable for its Florentine charm, and it is impossible to miss the two handsome sheets of water at the entrance to the Tuileries, while the garden itself is set off by two huge basins. The fountain nearest the Carrousel is round, with a shallow basin in the middle that rests on four curved corbels; the octagonal basin, on the other hand, has a single majestic jet of water. One fountain follows another along the flower-filled promenade of the Champs-Élysées beyond the Luxor obelisk in the Place de la Concorde: near the Espace Cardin, Duret's *Venus* carefully gathers her hair into a twist; the *Diana* in the Carré Marigny holds her robe of silver and wind; children dance on the Circus fountain near the Marigny Theater; and the Élysée fountain has an immense basin and two majestic spouts, one celebrating flowers and fruit, the other fishing.

The great succession of Parisian basins is impressive: that of the Champ-de-Mars; the theatrical waterfall in the Trocadéro gardens with its rockery, cascades and rivers running through the tall grass; the shallow basin at the Invalides with a plume-shaped

Animated by the violence of the water, Frémiet's horses belong to the admirable group The Four Corners of the World *in the Marco Polo Garden.*

fountain; the basin in the new gardens of the Arsenal, the one in Square Émile Chautemps admired by the Surrealist poets for its eccentricity and sensuality; the pond in the Parc Georges Brassens where stepping stones provide a passage through a profusion of exotic plants; the basin in the Jardin de l'Intendant; those in the Palais-Royal that create a sheet of falling spray.

Meanwhile, what is left of the parterres of water, the gold and silver falls of the French *Grand Siècle*? In *Les Raisons des forces mouvantes* (1615), Salomon de Caus examined twenty "questions" concerning water in gardens. He studied the various intellectual, emotional and optical effects, thereby making water a major component in French garden design.

For his part, Claude Mollet, in *Théâtre des plans et jardinages*, wrote that fountains and statuary should be vertical and rhythmic notes that "divide and enhance space, attract

The allegory of The Seine and Its Affluents
*adorns the Larche fountain, placed at the entrance to the Grand Palais
in 1910 (top). The graceful* Circus *fountain in the gardens
of the Champs-Élysées was created by sculptor Jean Barre (facing).
Many different varieties of birds inhabit the parks and
gardens of Paris (above). The Grande Cascade fountain in the
Parc de Saint-Cloud offers an amazing spectacle, called
Les Grandes-Eaux, on the second and fourth Sundays of the month,
from May to September (following page).*

attention and oblige the eye to stop and look at the other things that surround it." His was a solemn and idealized world in which terraced falls, majestic fountains, basins and cascades were not "natural," in other words, primitive and rocky; instead they were part of the architectural design. The Théâtre d'Eaux, or group of ornamental fountains, in the gardens of Versailles is probably the best example of this theory.

Achille Duchêne, who restored Saint-Cloud, agreed with this use of water and, although there is no castle to visit here, the spectacle of the Grandes Eaux should not be missed, even though only a part of its former cool beauty remains. First is the basin of the Swans — unfortunately now called the Horseshoe basin — that had "a farthingale slope, three fountains, two of which spout like darts." Several grassy terraces then lead up the allée de la Balustrade; from here the whole of Paris and the Grande Cascade are in view. This is another hydraulic marvel in which numerous ornamental fountains — jets, ripples, sheets, cascades, spouts — adorn the tiered structure. The top is decorated with two reclining figures, the *Seine* and the *Loire*, leaning on an urn from which spouts a torrent of water that fills stepped basins. The water descends from sheet to cascade until it forms a "deluge of crystal." In the park there are two basins with fountains and, in the middle of a large esplanade, a basin shaped like a four-leafed clover with twenty-four fountains that form a screen of water. Higher up across a second lawn lies the circular reservoir that provides water for the park fountains, adorned with the splendid Grande Gerbe.

Other marvels await at the Parc de Sceaux. Colbert had an immense amount of work done on the conduits, and the fountain-maker Le Jongleur joined his talents to those of Le Nôtre to produce one of the most imposing cascades

in France. The first basin from the château is circular, with two jets of water. It is fed by a system of cleverly camouflaged pumps that function every Sunday in summer. Next there is a succession of ledges, bordered with vertical sprays of water set in the lawns, that end at a basin surrounded by steps that lead to the Octogone basin. Thus a gigantic water staircase unfolds before our eyes.

When sculpted monuments become garden adornments such as fountains, ponds, staircases and railings, they play an active part in the aesthetics of the Parisian landscape, even if they are mutilated or mediocre, or no longer exist in their original setting. It is impossible to imagine the Luxembourg Gardens without its population of statues of the Ladies of France that frame the Grand Bassin, teaching History to the passing student. By the same token, the equestrian statue of Henry IV dominates the small Place Dauphine and the Square du Vert-Galant. And it is impossible to imagine the great vistas of the Place de la Concorde and the Champs-Élysées without Coustou's superb horses.

The statuary in the Tuileries embodies the political history of France from royalty to the Republic. Le Nôtre once erected two groups of classical figures representing war in its strength and peace in its wisdom — *Mars* and *Minerva* — and during the Regency the fragile French royalty was bolstered by a massive production of statues to its glory. The Convention, after lengthy debates as to whether to commission statues of heroes and martyrs of the Revolution, finally decided to bring into the city statuary from parks created under the *ancien régime*, such as Marly, Versailles and Sceaux. Napoleon I built the triumphal arch of his Grande Armée in the Carrousel courtyard, at the entrance of the palace and the gardens. Under the Restoration and later under Louis-Philippe,

In the Arènes de Lutèce, a woman in stone lost in her reading reflects the tranquility of a garden filled with history (facing).

new bas-reliefs and a row of "antique" marbles were added to the arch, and Napoleon III created the vast Cour Napoleon. After the palace was burned and the Commune suppressed, Parisian gardens sprouted numerous monuments exalting the leaders of the Republican left, such as the famous *Gambetta* and *Quand même*.

Between the two world wars, the production of monumental art slowed down and did not pick up until 1964, when the Minister for Arts and Culture, André Malraux, began to install the first works of his *Musée imaginaire*. Overnight, Paris was overrun with handcarts full of smiling nymphs, royal matrons, sightless ephebes, naked children and famous men whom the Parisians nicknamed "the

condemned." They were dumped in provincial museums and gardens while casts by Aristide Maillol were placed in the Jardin du Carrousel.

The direction of the National Heritage, after hesitating for a long time, recently decided to implement an ambitious policy for historical gardens, and the future of the Tuileries now appears to be assured. There is no question of giving up the idea of "garden galleries" that resulted in new sculptures and exhibitions by artists like Henry Moore (1979) and Richard Serra (1983); neverthless, the limiting concept of the Tuileries as an "open-air museum" that prevailed until very recently has been abandoned. This applies to all the major Parisian gardens.

A visitor standing before the Gallo-Roman ruins in Square Capitan in the attractive Arènes de Lutèce, or in front of the Philippe-Auguste stele in the Jardin Étienne Marcel, may feel a certain melancholy. There may be some regret for the garden figures of antiquity as reinterpreted by the eighteenth century; or the works of Falconet, who treated his statues (none of which have survived) like marble actors in a play about the pleasures and games of his century. There are, however, flowering areas of the capital where the *Seasons* dance with *Children*; a marble *Winter* and *Summer* encircle the Tuileries basin; *Autumn, Winter, Summer* and *Messidor* line the central avenue in this same garden; and *April* blooms in the middle of the basin in Square Galliéra.

Other noteworthy works include bronzes of *Arago* and *Ledru-Rollin* by David d'Angers in the Père-Lachaise cemetery; Bourdelle's *Gustave Eiffel* in the Champ-de-Mars; several bronzes by Coysevox in the Luxembourg Gardens; Rodin's sculptures in the gardens of his museum or the Montparnasse cemetery; Juan Miró's *L'Oiseau lunaire* in Square Blomet; Brancusi's *Kiss* in Montparnasse

*Generous and sensual in their nudity,
Maillol's women grace the lawns in the Tuileries (above).
In the refined vegetation of the
Ranelagh Garden, Meditation (1882) by Toni Noël (facing).*

cemetery; Picasso's *Head of a Woman* at the base of the Saint-Germain-des-Prés church; sculptures by Calder, Giacometti, Alicia Penalba and Van Thienen in the Parc Floral at Vincennes.

There is cause to regret, however, that Parisian gardens have not yet been cleared of mediocre late nineteenth- and early twentieth-century monumental art. Crowds of obscure celebrities and nymphs accompanied by sinister gentlemen in frock coats still encumber the view, and there are far too many patriotic celebrations in stone of Victorious France and monuments to Delacroix, Maupassant, Chopin, Gounod and Voltaire, not to mention the endless hymns to the *Defense of the Home* (Square d'Ajaccio) or to *Learning at a Mother's Knee* (Square Samuel Rousseau).

Parisian gardens are full of objects of art and culture, but they are also remarkable for their overall unity and harmony, for it is not so much the intrinsic quality of a statue that contributes to the beauty of a garden, but its careful placement. Where Carpeaux, for instance, meticulously organized the plants around the Observatory and used the freedom of sculpture in the round to make the feather-light sphere of the *Four Corners of the*

World turn in the sky, Rodin's massive, superb *Porte de l'Enfer* in the gardens of his museum looks as if it was placed there without topographical considerations. The *Bourgeois de Calais*, on the contrary, is isolated to set off its intensely moving monumentalness. In the winter, the ice in the Jardin Tino Rossi transforms Nicolas Schöffer's sculpture, *Chronos 10*, into a glittering crystal creation of subtle and ingenious mirrors. *Flora* descends from her chariot to spread Square Georges Cain with flowers. In the garden that runs alongside Saint-Germain-des-Prés there stands a monumental enameled stoneware portico manufactured at Sèvres for the 1900 Universal Exposition.

The first policy that encouraged the creation of public open spaces was inaugurated under Napoleon III, and it included the concept of furnishings, which were intended to make people temporarily forget the hardship of their lives by providing "hygiene and well-being."

The architect Gabriel Davioud, who created the best *fabriques*, still present in Parisian gardens — grottoes, rotundas, chapels, café-restaurants, kiosks, puppet theaters, and more utilitarian structures such as toilets, urinals, guard's houses and huts — also created the

One of the candy kiosks in the Luxembourg Gardens has been run with zeal by a mother and her daughter for thirty-seven years (top). In spring, large stone vases overflowing with flowers adorn the odd-shaped benches in the Champ-de-Mars (above).

earliest garden furnishings, including railings, lamp-posts with several branches, seats, metal barriers, and even advertisement boards. His style, shown in the engravings in Alphand's book introducing the new *Promenades de Paris*, was inspired by nature, with an added touch of exoticism. His famous "dragon-scaled domes" that crown numerous chalets and rotundas were so successful that the domes now sit atop newspaper kiosks, Morris advertising columns and the Wallace fountains. Furthermore, the design of each object varies according to the nobility of its surroundings. The spearheads on the railings of the Luxembourg are gilded; the gates at Monceau — also gilded — are wrought-iron marvels, whereas the railings around the Square du Temple are plain and functional. Similarly, the expensively wrought street lamps on the Champs-Élysées have three candelabra branches, while those in the more ordinary Oudry style have two sorts of brass lanterns: a round one for the center of Paris and a less ornate square one for the suburbs. The use of industrial materials — brick, brass, wrought iron — is characteristic of Davioud's work. The Napoleon III benches, for example, combine a sinuous cast-iron base with thick oak slats painted green to blend in with the environment.

This decorative picturesque style prefigures the École de Nancy that was to inspire the French art nouveau a few years later. Its utilitarian aesthetics result from the economic considerations of mass production. This technical aspect explains how a uniformity of style was able to survive right into the 1930s, when the shapes were simplified.

It was during this period that the administration of the Third Republic ordered those corolla-shaped wastepaper baskets, symbolic of the utilitarianism, negligence and the vandalism of the times, that still

exist in most Parisian gardens. But functionalism reached its culmination after the Second World War: cement or plastic garden furniture was strong, practical and easily replaceable — in other words, frequently awful.

To prevent the installation of this dull kind of furniture, Moreaux designed his own for Square René Le Gall and, using simple, inexpensive materials — concrete, pebbles, small stones imitating mosaics — he proved that it does not necessarily cost more to be creative. But his example was scarcely followed, and it was not until the prestigious operations of the 1970s and 1980s that anything other than mass-produced furniture began to appear in new Parisian gardens.

The sumptuous gates of Parc Monceau designed by Davioud appear to preciously guard the mysteries of the garden.

The classical gardener preferred to prune plants rather than train them. Watercolors of the Nymph fountain at Marly reveal the perfection of the topiary art as practiced by Louis XIV's gardeners. Trees trained into arches form covered walks that are as geometrically precise as a series of ribbed vaults. There is absolutely nothing supporting them; they are entirely sculpted in greenery. A synthesis of the French gardening style, *Traité de jardinage*, written by Dézallier d'Argenville in the early eighteenth century, abounds with sketches of topiary woods of great architectural virtuosity.

On the other hand, the "return to nature" preached by Rousseau and later by the nineteenth-century romantics, meant that nature was no longer controlled; it became instead the guiding force. Huts made of branches, hermitages nestling among the trees, green or flowering arbors for which the growing verdure was sometimes plaited began to appear, but there was little, if any, trained trelliswork.

It was, indeed, so scarce that one of Alphand's master gardeners, Edouard André, writing in 1879, went so far as to state that pergolas had played only a very minor role in French gardens. A few years later, however, a reversion to a geometric gardening style brought about the renaissance of trelliswork.

Yet there was no question of reviving the complicated topiary work of the *Grand Siècle*. According to the manifesto *Art des jardins* (1913) written by André Véra, economy and simplicity dictated that the simple pruning of yews, box and greenery had to suffice, as the restorations of historical gardens carried out by Achille Duchêne's workshop demonstrated. Nevertheless, trellises were used for decorative motifs and an occasional geometrical design, despite the economic restrictions.

These attempts have not all been successful. The gardens of Les Halles and the Parc de Belleville reveal just how perilous the design of a modern street lamp can be. But Philippe Starck's designs for the Parc de La Villette have a convincing sobriety: seats with pivoting bases and buried pedestals, trays combining wastepaper baskets, lighting and ashtrays, street lamps in the shape of long vertical cylinders.

Although Haussmann, Alphand and Davioud deserve credit for having invented furnishings that were adapted to the new public spaces, it is nevertheless unfortunate that they ignored the charming trelliswork used to create earlier arbors, bowers and pergolas. These were widely used during the Middle Ages and the Renaissance, but faded in popularity over the ensuing centuries.

The dead leaves on the public benches replace the strollers once autumn arrives (above). Pretty chairs with an old-fashioned charm can be found in the Luxembourg Gardens among chairs dating from the 1950s (facing).

This change in taste and technique explains the appearance of the sublime rose gardens at Bagatelle and L'Haÿ-les-Roses, at Malmaison and the Jardins Albert Kahn. The ancient art of the trellis-makers was once again required to train climbing roses — sometimes mixed with Irish ivy or Virginia creeper — to cover bowers, fences, arbors, pergolas, or covered avenues. In the rose gardens designed by Duchêne and Forestier, the austere "textbook" geometry comes fragrantly to life.

Twenty years later, Moreaux was inspired by these earlier creations when he designed the four bowers of his symmetrical garden in Square René Le Gall: even though the dome-shaped trellises are made of concrete, from the month of May or June the climbing roses transform them into lush tiaras of fragrant greenery.

Trelliswork is once again visible in Parisian gardens after being eclipsed by the preponderance of the "green space" over the last thirty years. In Les Halles the trellises have been given the form of animals to please the children. In the Jardin de l'Arsenal some facilities are disguised with greenery. Used in their own right, they divide the garden of trellises at La Villette. As luxurious additions, they form a handsome covered avenue in Belleville and, with even greater magnificence, a stairway of greenery in Square Paul Langevin. In this square, against the wall of the former École Polytechnique, a modern horseshoe-shaped double flight of stairs leads to a terrace overlooking the garden. Covered in climbing knotgrass, its dreamlike quality is reflected in the theater of greenery framing Childebert's fountain that forms the main area of the garden.

Enveloped in viburnum, the staircase in the Square Langevin forms a strange sculpture of greenery.

Fountains, basins, statues, kiosks, balustrades, trellises and picturesque *fabriques* in the shape of rocks, grottoes, streams or footbridges are obligatory garden ornaments. Beyond their decorative or functional role, they have a double vocation: to differentiate a garden from nature, and to give it what specialists call "scale." Furthermore, they embody an essential principle: at the origins of art there is always artifice — a *fabrique*.

However large a garden or a park, its area is limited, whereas nature is not. This leads to a seemingly insurmountable contradiction between the dream and the reality. How can what is by definition a limited space be made to appear infinite?

These kinds of questions have received different answers throughout the history of gardening. Le Nôtre, and Tschumi to some extent, chose to make the artifice visible at each step, by sectioning the area into a network of vegetable, sculptural or architectural events, and by using perspective to link the small-scale elements — woods and statues for Le Nôtre, follies for Tschumi — to an illusion of the infinite. For their part the creators of picturesque landscapes attempted to present a "beautiful nature" that is hardly any different from the nature that surrounds

it. Yet they created and placed *fabriques* in the parks to denote the presence of man and the necessity of art. And, in the words of contemporary landscapist Bernard Lassus, they attempted to make the "unmeasurable" enter the "measurable," by drawing the "exterior" into the "interior" of the garden.

"Gardeners are not only Botanists but also Painters and Philosophers," according to the great eighteenth-century landscape-architect William Chambers. Does this mean that a place that contains only greenery does not deserve to be called a garden? To this question, the gardens of Paris, which are intellectual as much as material creations and where the vegetation is allied to the mineral, provide an answer.

Magnificently fused with the vegetation, the enameled sandstone portico at the Square Félix Desruelles was manufactured at Sèvres for the Exhibition of 1990 (top). The Triumph of Bacchus decorates the fountain created by Dalou for the Auteuil greenhouses (above). The luxuriant Parc des Missions Étrangères is one of the intimate and secret gardens of the seventh arrondissement (following page).

7

UNUSUAL GARDENS

Among the great teaching gardens, promenades, malls, avenues, squares, parks and woods of Paris are many areas of greenery that are revealed only to those whom the poet Léon-Paul Fargue described in his *Piéton de Paris* as "people of leisure, in other words those who have time to spare and who love Paris."

It is a pleasure to escape the main avenues and tourist itineraries and set off through streets, passages and courtyards in search of these unusual gardens.

Far from the urban turmoil of Paris, the memory of a more pastoral city comes to life in the evocative names of these old avenues: rural names like rue Notre-Dame-des-Champs (Our Lady of the Fields), rue du Chemin-Vert (Green Path), rue de la Cerisaie (Cherry Orchard) and rue Bois-le-Vent (Windy Wood); colorful ones like rue du Champfleury (Flowering Field), rue du Point-du-Jour (Daybreak), rue du Pont-aux-Biches (Doe Bridge); and even a reminder of the dangers that beset our ancestors in rue de la Brèche-aux-Loups (Wolf-Breach).

These secret gardens belong to schools, institutes, embassies and religious communities, or they once belonged to private houses and villas and are now shared by condominiums, although they are still embellished with the rose and ivy-filled urns of the *belle époque*. These unlikely gardens lead to a Paris that is like an illuminated land register: cours de l'Etoile-d'Or (Golden Star), passage du Sud (Southern Passage), rue du Soleil and rue de la Lune (Sun and Moon streets).

The past lives on. A shaft of sunlight, the shadow of a sequoia tree, the medallions on a façade, the mosaics in a passageway or a worn statue can fire the imagination to reconstruct a fragment of the history of France. Dare to push open a door or a gate; beyond is a magic land of opulent parks, enclosed squares, paths, flowering courtyards, groves of trees, benches, flower pots overflowing with geraniums, rose laurel, melilot and veronica.

Of course these gardens are not always easy to visit: some of them belong to the state, like the gardens of the Élysée Palace, which are open to the President's guests on July 14, and once a year to the public. Some belong to religious communities and are only partially open to the public; others are strictly private and their fierce concierges frown on the visitor who forgets to introduce himself or to praise the beauty of the spot.

*Well hidden in the sixteenth arrondissement,
the Sainte-Périne Garden is planted with handsome trees, while the
flowers attract splendid white butterflies (above).
The garden at the Rodin Museum has beds and charming alleys with
rose bushes and sculptures by the artist (facing).*

A single walk can begin to unravel the labyrinth of interlocking itineraries and reveal the complicated harmony underlying the uniqueness of Paris. Getting lost is worth it for the sheer pleasure of finding one's way again.

Cemeteries are perhaps the strangest of Parisian gardens, for they are places both of burial and of life. Throughout the year they are inhabited by diverse tribes of stray cats with phosphorescent eyes — known as "graveyard cats" — that are fed discreetly by elderly ladies.

Time seems to stand still among the funeral monuments. The click of ghostly secateurs may be heard through the rustling of the branches, or there may be a glimpse of a silhouette raking the avenues. This spectral scene suggests the presence of a mysterious, unending merry-go-round that comes to life only in the depths of the night. Yet even if time seems to have stopped, history still rules in these strange gardens.

Sophora, horse chestnut, quince and plane trees shade the elegant parterres in the garden of the Institut Catholique, located in rue d'Assas (top). Protected by a border of boxwood, white lilies blossom in the basin of this garden, also known as the Carmelite's garden (above). A statue of the Virgin beneath the trees in the Babylone garden inspires peace and meditation (facing).

The Picpus cemetery contains the most painful memories of all the Parisian cemeteries. It belongs to the order of the Congrégation des Sœurs de l'Adoration Perpétuelle and is sometimes called La Fayette's cemetery, for he is buried there; Americans in Paris celebrate his memory every fourth of July. But it has a darker side, for during the Terror the bodies beheaded by the guillotine were unceremoniously dumped there. Purchased later by the Salm family, the enclosure was divided into two sections, with 1, 298 tombs on one side and plants on the other. The names on the tombs include families whose ancestors were victims of the Terror: Chateaubriand, La Rochefoucauld, Noailles, Rohan, Montmorency. In the shady and peaceful other side lie the remains of the martyred poet André Chénier.

A garden both of anguish and of glory, the Picpus cemetery is one of the most moving gardens in Paris, and one of the most beautiful, situated at the end of an irregularly paved courtyard behind a high wooden door. Flocks of starlings from nearby Square Saint-Éloi chatter in the flower-filled parterres and among the sycamore, ash and fruit trees.

Compared with the small enclosure of the Picpus cemetery, Père-Lachaise, which covers 109 acres, is immense. Situated at the intersection of the three villages in the twentieth arrondissement — Belleville, Ménilmontant and Charonne — it is the largest and most frequently visited Parisian cemetery. Its abundant vegetation and romantic avenues and statues make it a wonderfully picturesque garden, especially in autumn.

Père-Lachaise stands on a hill on which, in the twelfth century, the bishop of Paris owned a vineyard and wine press. Until as late as the early nineteenth century it was referred to as "Parisian countryside," and walks like the allée Duée are as narrow as a country lane. It was, in fact, the site of the "Folie Regnault" before it became a Jesuit rest home. The adolescent Louis XIV is said to have watched the riots of the *Fronde* (1648-1653) from there, and after the Revolution it was given to the city of Paris under the name of "Mont-Louis." But it was more commonly known as the "House of Père La Chaise" after the zealous confessor to the king who turned the site into a French-style garden for the comfort of his flock. In 1804 Frochot, the prefect of Paris, transformed it into a necropolis and commissioned the architect Brongniart, who designed the Paris Stock Exchange, to draw up the plans. In 1805 burials began to be conducted in this garden that combines an English landscaped park and a French-style garden.

Today Père-Lachaise is not only one of the most beautiful cemeteries in the world, but also the largest park in Paris. The 5,300 trees include species of maple, ash, thuja and chestnut alongside plane, box, beech, lime, robinia, heart-shaped alder, sophora and hickory trees that turn glorious gold in autumn. The dew lightly covers the area behind the purple beech in the twenty-seventh division of the cemetery, where the

A pleasant pergola covered with a young vine stands by a double hedge of hazel trees and gooseberry bushes in the Babylone Garden (above). It is pleasant to wander in the shade of the chestnut trees and admire the carefully organized flower beds in the Parc des Missions Étrangères (facing).

Commune made its last stand from May 21 to 28, 1871. It was then transformed from a place of rest into a terrifying battlefield in which the amphoras and crosses failed to stop the hail of bullets. The government troops sent from Versailles by Adolphe Thiers — who is, ironically, now buried in the cemetery in a huge square mausoleum — fired on the unarmed Parisian workers and students. Their bodies were buried in pits dug under the wall that now carries their names, in the northeast corner of the cemetery.

Some of the most impressive figures of this massacre lie here: Eugène Pottier, author of *Internationale*, and Jean-Baptiste Clément, whose song *Le Temps des cérises* is dedicated to the young woman he loved who died at the barricades.

Every year on November 11 the wall of the *Fédérés* is covered in bouquets of roses, and the monument to the dead is saluted to the sound of the *Chant des Morts* in solemn commemoration of all the martyrs of France. Near the blood-stained wall is also a monument to the victims of Nazism. One million people have been buried in Père-Lachaise to date. And yet this cemetery is more like a "hill of inspiration" on which sculptures drawn from both antiquity and nature are assembled in extraordinary profusion. It contains every possible style of funerary monument: plain tombstones, pompous crypts from the Haussmann era, flamboyant Gothic tombs, wrought iron, granite or marble tombs signed by sculptors and architects such as Guimard, Garnier, Viollet-le-Duc, David d'Angers and Rude. There are unusual works such as Félix de Beaujour's sixteen-meter-high cone, the ogival dais of Héloïse and Abelard's mausoleum, and Allan Kardec's dolmen. Near the crematorium, the columbarium resembles a huge "library of urns."

With one million visitors a year, Père-Lachaise is the fifth most frequented spot in Paris after the Eiffel Tower, Notre Dame, the Arc de Triomphe and the Jardin des Plantes. But this "city of the dead" has not escaped the inevitable aging that afflicts all gardens. Architect Patrick Berger and landscapist Gilles Clément were entrusted with refurbishing the cemetery in 1989; their plan is to thin out the vegetation and to recreate the wooded charm of Brongniart's original design.

All religious communities traditionally had adjoining gardens: the monastic kitchen garden fed the monks, the medicinal garden cured their ills and the flower garden decorated their altars. This is why all the old Parisian hospitals have gardens.

The garden of the Mosque, located at the heart of the fifth arrondissement, is a small Hispano-Moorish paradise. Abundant wisteria falls in clusters on the beautiful paving of the patio, where shadows and silence reign.

The history of the hospital of Hôtel-Dieu and its gardens is closely linked to that of Notre-Dame de Paris. These gardens once extended along both banks of the Seine, hence the name of the "pont au double," or "double bridge." A document dating from 1353 reveals that the monks of the Hôtel-Dieu had to "gather herbs and fruit" so that "said provost and citizens should give them as alms in God's name to the poor children." The garden of the Hôtel-Dieu was regularly cultivated until its disappearance during Haussmann's construction projects. When the Hôtel-Dieu was rebuilt between 1866 and 1878, gardens were created and the Square Charlemagne was planted.

Just inside the entrance a handsomely planted vista extends through the center of the buildings. It consists of a wide, paved courtyard full of flowers, followed by a garden with ornamental basins that is reached by climbing a monumental staircase. Peristyle courtyards, arcades, and stone balustrades and pavings give the garden a Florentine look. The main courtyard was created in the French style with a fountain, a maze, clipped box borders and statues by Dupuytren; the second garden has generous flower boxes that add bright spots of color to this attractive example of the "hygienist" style. An occasional kestrel flutters down from the Notre-Dame gargoyles to hover like a Holy Spirit, wings and tail outspread, under the trees that dot the tiny lawn, or a noisy jay from the walnut trees growing on the other side of the cathedral loses itself among the flamboyant colors of the flowers.

In front of the Pagoda cinema, formerly the reception pavilion for the Chinese legation, a charming garden was created with Japanese anemones, bamboos, maples and a rare ginkgo biloba.

The largest and most beautiful Parisian hospital garden, La Pitié-Salpêtrière, lies on the opposite bank of the Seine, near the Austerlitz station. It is reserved, like that of the Hôtel-Dieu, for patients and their visitors.

The Pitié-Salpêtrière establishment covers eighty-two acres of land, thirty acres of which are gardens. Although they now are part of the same complex, they were once two separate hospitals, and their histories are very different.

The Pitié hospital, created by Marie de' Medici in 1612, was a refuge for beggars and homeless people who were housed there against their will — hence their name, "The Confined." When Louis XIV decided to create a vast hospital network in Paris with the title of "Hôpital Général," La Pitié became its administrative center. It was demolished in 1912 and replaced by the present hospital. An avenue bordered with flower beds and flowering shrubs leads to the entrance. The seven to eight thousand plants are primarily summer flowers that give off a delightful fragrance in the evenings. Starting in spring, the forsythia, weigelia, guelder roses, spiraea with small white flowers and privet hedges around the buildings perfume the air.

Salpêtrière, the largest hospital in Paris, was also a place of "confinement for the poor," and by the late seventeenth century it became a detention center for women of "low life" and even for women whose husbands or fathers would no longer pay for their upkeep. In 1796 the hospital was given the task of caring for the mentally ill, and Pinel and Charcot came there to work. The buildings have an austere grandeur; the design and amplitude of the gardens that extend from courtyard to courtyard make them especially beautiful. The main courtyard behind a gateway at 47 boulevard de l'Hôpital includes some Judas trees and a Lebanese cedar. The lawns are edged with box trees and a paved central avenue leads to the chapel of Saint-Louis-de-la-Salpêtrière. A park with five hundred trees stands at the end of the Cour Lassay. Lower down is the asphalt hospital walk on which the

In the garden of the École des Beaux-Arts is the Cour du Mûrier and its wonderful octagonal fountain (top). This meditative garden, paved with lovely stones imported from Japan, is hidden behind the walls of the Unesco building (above).

*The Cité Fleurie is an Eden of vegetation in
the center of Paris. Twenty-nine artists' studios open onto exuberant
climbing rose bushes and Japanese quince trees (above).*

doctor in Agnès Varda's film *Cléo de cinq à sept* parked his car; it is seven o'clock on a spring evening and the sun is still shining on the lawns.

In the heart of Paris, the former École Polytechnique, the École des Beaux-Arts, the Institut Catholique, and the École Normale on rue d'Ulm above the Panthéon form a belt of pedagogical, artistic and cultural institutions. Their gardens may be quite simple, yet they nonetheless have the secret and lively charm of places where people go to exchange ideas or meditate.

The most important establishment for religious education in France is the Institut Catholique at 21 rue d'Assas. It has two gardens, both of which are tranquil and discreet. The main courtyard is very simple, with fine gravel, flower boxes, a few chestnut trees, some Virginia creeper, alcoves of box tree, a small fountain, and benches. The other garden — a huge, beautiful one, and without a doubt the largest private garden in Paris — is rarely open to the public.

The Institute was the site of some of the worst crimes during the massacres of September 1792, and the victims are commemorated on the perron of the seminary building with the

engraving *Hic ceciderunt*. More than one hundred priests were murdered and their bodies thrown down a well. Their remains were later buried in the Chapel of the Martyrs; its Italian-style wood dome dominates the large park full of trees, well-maintained lawns and flower-filled basins where young seminarists meditate and occasionally celebrate Mass. The small garden of the main courtyard has an air of charitable sweetness in the silence that reigns among the trees. The moment is a magical one. It almost seems possible to hear the ghostly voices of Bossuet, Bourdaloue, Lacordaire and Maritain. And when the stars are out, Pascal's ghost seems to be waiting for an eclipse under the gables of what is now the archive library. The scent of the famous liquorice plants grown by the Carmelites wafts from the grass, enhancing the mood of peaceful meditation.

In the courtyard of the Hôtel de Rohan, just off boulevard Saint-Germain, stones from ancient buildings have been transformed into a charming small bench (top). Behind the porch of the Hôtel de Châtillon in the Marais, the sun plays over the shadow of the stones and the branches of a catalpa (above).

An attractive public park containing currant bushes and apple, cherry and walnut trees has recently opened on the rue de Babylone on the site of the former kitchen gardens of the sisters of Saint-Vincent-de-Paul. It was baptized "Jardin de Babylone" after the street named for Bernard de Sainte Thérèse, bishop of Babylon and founder of the Missions Étrangères Seminary. Wood pigeons, collared turtle doves and swifts come from the many gardens nearby, such as Square Récamier with its shady woodland plants, Square Boucicaut and the Rodin Museum.

Not far away, at 105 rue du Bac, horse chestnuts, white poplars and magnificent Japanese cherry trees fill the Square des Missions Étrangères. A statue of Chateaubriand, who lived at 120 rue du Bac from 1838 to his death in 1848, stands in their shadows. He was a neighbor of Madame Récamier, who lived in the Abbaye-aux-Bois close by. He wrote *Vie de Rancé* here, as if the presence of the religious communities gave him a spiritual strength.

Still in rue du Bac, at number 128, the superb garden of the Missions Étrangères Seminary created in 1663 can be visited (by request only).

Other meditative gardens can be found at the Mosque, located just south of the Latin Quarter, opposite Square du Puits-de-l'Ermite and its willow and white mulberry trees. They were designed between 1922 and 1926, as was the Muslim Institute. One of the gardens, with fig and cherry trees growing in an empty lot perfumed with mint, surrounds the Grand Patio to the right of the religious buildings. The garden in the main courtyard is magnificent. A heavy eucalyptus, walnut and padouk wood door leads to a few steps framed by a stunning gallery of pink marble columns. Whatever the weather, even the darkest

corners are washed in light. Two small, white Moorish fountains with narrow rectangular basins are set into the turquoise mosaic floor; there are two similar fountains farther along, in the small courtyards on either side of the conference hall.

Tiny flowering checkerboard-shaped gardens bordered in clipped lavender are also enclosed in the floor mosaic. Beds full of exotic plants grow along the edges, and handsome wisteria and white rambling roses cover an arcade. The overall effect is one of astonishing light.

Back in the intellectual center of Paris on the left bank, there are modestly proportioned gardens that have nevertheless welcomed some of the greatest thinkers and nourished their

In the Bastille area, the Cour du Bel Air abounds with flowers and is often bathed in a radiant light (above).

Arts is at 14 rue Bonaparte in the sixth arrondissement. The nearby Seine and the Pont des Arts and the Pont-Neuf are in view. Two hundred years ago the Beaux-Arts building was a private townhouse presented to one of Josephine's nieces by Napoleon. Two centuries before that, it was the site of Queen Margot's palace and gardens. A basin filled with goldfish and a fountain in the center stands in the middle of the Cour du Mûrier. Clipped hedges and beds of greenery underline the austerity of the site, framed by buildings and arcades that are illuminated at night. Prix de Rome winners such as Ingres and Baltard came to chat or sketch in the Cour du Mûrier — named after the mulberry tree planted there shortly after the Revolution.

The seventh arrondissement, where many government ministries are located, contains two unusual Japanese gardens. The first, the Unesco garden in Place de Fontenoy, offers an amazing oriental landscape. Designed by American landscape sculptor Isamu Noguchi, it contains hundreds of plum, cherry and magnolia trees, bamboo, eighty tons of rocks brought from Japan, a stream, a lake and a bridge, all hidden behind the Unesco building. An ideogram for "peace" is carved on a fountain that springs from the largest rock. A magnificent mosaic by Bazaine stands opposite.

The second garden, at 57 bis rue de Babylone, is known to all cinema-lovers: it complements the reception pavilion built for the Chinese Legation in 1905. The building was later turned into a cinema, the Pagoda, and classified as a national monument in 1973. Abandoned for a time, this garden was replanted in its original oriental style. Film buffs meet here in front of the lovely façade decorated with blue, green, red and gold stoneware surrounded by bamboo,

imaginings with their shade, perfumes and touches of rusticity.

The garden of the École Normale Supérieure is composed of small flowering beds surrounded by box trees and a basin with a pleasant fountain that in spring reaches up to the flowers of one of the two Japanese plum trees. It is easy to imagine young people, unaware that they would later become the glory of their age, enjoying this peaceful garden, former students such as Henri Bergson, Jean-Paul Sartre, Michel Foucault, Raymond Aron, Louis Pasteur, Fustel de Coulanges, Charles Péguy, Romain Rolland, Jean Giraudoux, Jules Romains and Léopold Sédar Senghor.

The École Nationale Supérieure des Beaux-

By the first days of May, lilac, hawthorn, laburnum, spirea, seringa and pyracantha perfume the gardens of Paris.

maples, Japanese anemones and a gingko biloba.

Finally, in the sixteenth arrondissement, Robert Bazelaire created a water garden, rockwork and bamboo garden for the Hôtel Heidelbach-Guimet, an annex of the Asiatic Art Museum.

Throughout Paris, there are still some alleyways leading to small cottages and more or less wild gardens that housed artists and craftsmen before and after the Second World War: the Cité Véron near the Moulin-Rouge in the north of Paris, where Jacques Prévert, Boris Vian and Albert Diato lived; a number of quiet streets around Père-Lachaise; the inner courtyards of the Marais district; the small gardens of the Cité de la Moskowa; and the

cottages at the Peupliers postern gate. But little remains of these charming courtyards and gardens. Real estate developers purchased these glorified spaces and have profited from the memory of those who once worked there. Cité Verte, at 147 rue Léon-Maurice-Nordmann, is a good example. The paved avenue between the loquat and cherry trees planted by the sculptor Scarpa during the war gives an idea of what the Cité used to be. The pale green corkscrew staircase that he used to climb is still there, as is the large shelf of plaster on which he and his friends used to sit and chat in good weather. Henry Moore came to use the foundry, which no longer exists. The avenue has been widened and the edges close to the walls are scattered with fern, grasses and colorful flowers. The old district, with its acacias and hollyhocks, is about to be lost; it should have

The Poet's Garden, an oasis of calm in a busy area, pays homage to the great French poets. Beneath the trees stands Rodin's sculpture of Victor Hugo, one of his finest works (above). Gamay and pinot noir grapes are planted in the Montmartre vineyard, which, strangely enough, faces north. The grapes are therefore harvested late and a festival takes place in October (following page).

been saved. Soon all this will be no more than a memory preserved in the branches of the surrounding trees. Opposite, modern houses alternate with country-like homes and beds of greenery leading to boulevard Arago.

Beautiful chestnut trees four rows deep line boulevard Arago. The gate of the Cité Fleuri at number 65 opens to reveal a charming garden. About thirty artists now live there peacefully after waging a successful battle to save this site built from materials recovered from the 1878 Exposition. The conflict between artists and rapacious speculators hit the headlines in 1973 and mobilized the public. Thanks to Henri Cadiou, his wife, César Domela and Bram Van Velde, the rows of houses covered in Virginia creeper, wisteria and honeysuckle give

the impression of a bit of countryside set miraculously in the middle of Paris. The garden is planted with many species of trees, including a clerodendron that a harpist is said to have brought back from Japan, a one-hundred-year-old lime tree saved from the woodchopper's axe by the local artists, a sour apple tree, a cherry tree that produces Morello cherries in July, and a quince tree that provides kilos of quinces, transformed into jam each year by the residents. Great quantities of roses and impatiens grow around the basins.

Almost one hundred years ago Rodin met his trusted friend Limet here, and Bourdelle, Maillol and Despiau were frequent visitors. Gauguin brought his Tahitian paintings and impatiently awaited the judgment of his friend Daniel de Monfreid, who was a resident here.

Cité Fleuri was and still is visited by many foreign artists, among them the sculptor Soudbidine — who worked in the studio where Chaliapin sang and Pavlova and Karsavina danced — and the Spaniard Benito who painted the portrait of Paul Poiret, decorated Gloria Swanson's Paris home and illustrated American *Vogue*. Modigliani received Mexican painter Angel Zarraga in studio number 9. During the Second World War studio number 18 housed a library of books banned by the Nazis; in 1940 the place was pillaged and artists like the sculptor Simon paid for their participation in the Resistance with their lives.

Close by, on the site of a tennis court, a new garden has just been created: Square Henry-de-Montherlant.

A number of studios were built at the end of the last century from lightweight materials, often by the artists themselves, in what was then the outskirts of Paris: Montmartre in the north, and the fourteenth and fifteenth

Dead leaves are carried aloft by the wind before being strewn on the ground in magical collages.

arrondissements in the south. The Bateau-Lavoir on rue Ravignan, destroyed by fire in 1970 and rebuilt in 1978 to house modern artists; the Ruche at 2 passage Dantzig, the center of the "Paris School"; and Cité Fleuri in the fourteenth arrondissement — these historic sites, which have narrowly escaped development, have become fashionable among the bourgeoisie. These artistic dwellings have therefore been transformed into more profitable apartment houses or into "villas," where the gardens have kept some of their former poetry. These villas, like Villa Hallé, Villa Brune and Villa Seurat, are usually short, dead-end alleys closed off by high ivy-clad walls.

Villa Adrienne at 19 avenue du Général-Leclerc reflects the undefinable melancholy and Proustian atmosphere common to these gardens. Nothing in the busy boulevard and intense traffic nearby suggests the tranquility that lies so close by. In the middle of the large courtyard bordered on three sides by two-story brick buildings and on the fourth by villas with gardens, extends a profusely planted rectangular garden. It was designed in the landscapist style with flower beds, tall trees (birch, poplar, weeping willow) and winding paths, while the private gardens on the fourth side are smaller and more varied. Its enclosed form suggests that of a convent and the Villa Adrienne, constructed in 1883, may even appear to have no life at all. Yet with the swirling movement of the willow catkins, the tiny, almost triangular birch leaves, the rustling of the poplars and the blossoming beds, the villa regains its proud and enigmatic

*Wild alleys bordered by baroque tombs,
neoclassical sepulchral stones and antique urns beneath the
shade of majestic trees confer a strange and
melancholic beauty on the Père-Lachaise cemetery (above).*

beauty. Who was Adrienne, who built this house and garden on the site of a property in Montrouge owned by the Duc de La Vallière, nephew of the famous duchess? History stops there: unfortunately, we know nothing about this mysterious woman.

A few steps away, opposite 63 rue Hallé, extends the villa of the same name under the shadows of trees from another century. From afar only the violet shadow of a wisteria in bloom is visible. The villa is a group of small one- or two-story houses, with gardens front and back strung along a green and flowering path that is barely fifty meters long by three meters wide. It looks like a village street that ends at a small square. The gardens have a few chestnut trees, limes, acacias and enough flowers to create the impression of being miles away from a major city.

In this place, as in the strange village in rue Georges-Lardennois near Buttes-Chaumont, the city appears as a series of images, thoughts, and sensations. It is a world that has exploded into fragments, an illusion, a dream machine. The light that shines down from the wrought-iron balcony is a different color from the light that seeps from under the tapestry of greenery. Climbing plants take on giant proportions: the Virginia creeper seems to be too green and the wisteria too beautiful. Villa Hallé offers a dream landscape built from utterly simple rustic elements. The small flowering gardens, the paving stones and the luxuriant wisteria enrich this fantasy.

Even though plants in Paris grow in tiny, uneven and frequently inhospitable plots of land, they nevertheless perpetuate the French rural tradition. This is especially true for the vines growing on Butte Montmartre, in the Babylone gardens, in the Parc de Bercy, on the slopes of Belleville, in the Parc Georges

Brassens and in the Parc Floral, as well as the hundreds of small trellises in private gardens. Just as the city is decked in roses with the coming of summer, the vines flourish triumphantly in autumn. Vines first appeared in Lutetia during the Gallo-Roman period, and they were grown widely throughout the Middle Ages, only to almost disappear in the eighteenth century in the face of competition from building speculation and other French wines. In the sixteenth century there were still vineyards in Montmartre, where the residents were mostly vineyard workers, but vines also grew in the rue des Morillons, rue des Vignes and rue Vineuse, and in the districts of the Épinettes and the Goutte-d'Or. Considered a great Île-de-France vintage in the fourteenth century, the Parisian wine is now a "petit vin" for local consumption. A grape-picking festival is held every year in October on the butte: a procession winds through the enclosure that contains two thousand stocks. The wine, pressed in the cellars of the town hall of the eighteenth arrondissement, is auctioned off on behalf of the "social works" of the butte. As night falls the vineyards of rue Saint-Vincent are lit with a crimson flush and the distant city seems to disappear.

The thirty-five kilometers of railway lines that form the Petite-Ceinture are a strange mixture of tunnels, passages, railings, gratings full of thistles, black nightshade, red nettle, and false acacias that line the route encircling Paris. Once a method of transporting "merchandise in times of peace" and "men and ammunition in times of war," the line was laid between 1852 and 1867. The Petite-Ceinture was transformed into a public transportation system in 1883 when the railway lines and marshalling yards of the Grande-Ceinture were laid out. It finally closed in 1934 when it was made obsolete by the metro. Today it is a garden run wild, but a steam engine still puffs its way between the East, North and Lyon train stations. In its southern section the train whistle blows only once every two months or so, to the great delight of people leaning over the parapets of the bridges above. In these sections of the fourteenth and fifteenth arrondissements, the Petite-Ceinture forms a surprisingly open area, one with a countrified and even woodland atmosphere.

The long, narrow furrow that encircles Paris like a hollow fence includes the railway as part of the foundation rites of a past reality. The trembling acacias, the tufted vetch, the feverfew, the royal nettle, the wild grass and even the rails contribute to this mysterious topology. From one of the small bridges above, the tracks seem to plunge far beyond the vanishing point. It contains a little of

everything, and forms a sort of universal botany, a compendium of the plant world. Even though the regularity of the planted trees defines a space that could be called "a garden," the anarchy of the plants and grasses suggests instead a savannah, a forest or a bedlam of greenery sprouted from strange seeds: there are incredible thickets of young bamboo, wild roses with verdigris shadows, snakelike digitalis, overgrown flower beds, barbarea, pepperwort, sow thistle and wild chervil.

Thus soars the imagination, in dreams of the Parisian gardens that existed, vanished, then reappeared in a profusion of checkerboard patterns, spirals and filigrees of light and shadow. Is it not in this tracery of old and new gardens that the strong, transparent light displays Paris's extraordinary depths?

*Arcades and balustrades predominate in
the lovely garden of the Hôtel-Dieu (above). The first level of
the Eiffel Tower overlooks the sober and grandiose
Champ-de-Mars, bordered with secret gardens (following page).*

8

ART NOUVEAU
AND ART DECO

However sophisticated gardens may be, they are nonetheless perishable. This fragility makes them even more precious, and bestows on the most beautiful of them the moving grace of a subtle art under the constant threat of destruction.

In the past the precarious character of parks and gardens was taken for granted and, since the idea of a national heritage had not yet been conceived, each age took liberties with the creations of the previous one, liberties that would be unthinkable today. Parks and gardens were especially vulnerable to these cruel transformations, which occurred most often during revolutions, or when urban growth suddenly made their land valuable. Thus, like the follies built on the outskirts of the city at the end of the eighteenth century, most of the gardens belonging to the private houses in the Marais and the Faubourg Saint-Jacques disappeared, while royal parks passed into the public domain to suffer countless changes and mutilations.

Closer to the present day, however, there were many properly preserved gardens, before the art of gardening entered a serious decline in the middle of this century. The period that runs from the 1890s to the 1920s — in other words from art nouveau to art deco — along with the Second Empire and contemporary design, are therefore the most interesting insofar as Parisian horticultural areas are concerned. During this time Paris acquired major new parks: the gardens of the Trocadéro and the Champ-de-Mars were redesigned for the Universal Expositions of 1889, 1900 and 1937. This period also produced gardens such as Square René Le Gall and Parc Kellerman, in a less elaborate but nevertheless sophisticated style, with the result that today a visitor in search of the spirit of gardening that reigned when Montparnasse was the center of modern art has almost too great a choice.

The word geometry, taken in its broadest sense, can be used to summarize those inventive years that were cut in two by the horror of the Great War. As with painting — in which the luminous dissolution of forms in Monet's last canvases was countered by Cézanne's firm architectural shapes, and later still, by the decomposition of space in cubism or the neoplasticism of De Stijl and Le Corbusier — the evolution of garden design led to a gradual rejection of a "soft landscape" that had become more and more academic, in favor of compositions that used axes, straight lines and precisely delineated volumes.

After the death of Barillet-Deschamps in 1871, Alphand, appointed to the prefecture of Paris by Adolphe Thiers, President of the Third Republic (even though he had worked for the Second Empire), imposed his ideas and an engineer's regularity of form on Parisian gardens. Superficially there were no changes. The "landscapist" style that had been developed with such brilliance by Barillet-Deschamps continued to dominate Parisian squares, avenues and parks.

Like Haussmann, Alphand, as director of the "embellishment of Paris," reduced the urban landscape to a strict pattern. In *Les Promenades de Paris* (1867-1873), Alphand (who was conspicuously absent from Barillet-Deschamps's funeral) stated that, depending on the district, it was essential to use a particular design for a square, a specific style of railings and garden furniture, and a predetermined selection of plants and trees. In other words, even though he shared in the invention of the landscapist style, and anticipated the industrial logistics that would inspire Gropius and Le Corbusier, Haussmann's former second-in-command had reverted to the stylistic immobility of his master. This implied a scant respect for history and negation of the *genius loci* in the name of

The four small arbors in the Square René Le Gall, a hidden garden in the Gobelins area, are covered each summer with luxuriant, sweet-smelling climbing roses (facing).

a "grandiose simplicity" that could only please a bourgeoisie more enamored of Bouguereau than Manet. Gone were the variety, the mixtures of color, the adjustments or additions to an urban layout that had been subtly wrought by time, fashion, the haphazard growth of the population and geographical irregularities. They were replaced with order, a hierarchical tidiness devoted to hygiene, and a practicality that strove toward standardization and homogeneity.

Édouard André's interpretation of the landscapist style explains this rationalization in technical language: "Instead of simply leveling the surface of the terracing, one studied the art of remodeling the ground. The centers of lawns were sunk, the beds of shrubbery were raised, the trees were made to stand out and beds of flowers, always

elliptical and slightly raised, were 'leaned' against them." The word "always" reveals the dogmatism of Alphand's landscape theories: these characteristics of the horticultural creations of the Second Empire had been suppressed by the genius of Barillet-Deschamps. Once he was gone, they reappeared.

The Parc Montsouris is a revealing example. Far be it for us to deny this site its power to enchant. The elegance of the tall trees, the noble curves of the avenues, the variety of vistas, the undulating splendor of the lawns, the beauty of the grottoes and cascades, as well as the public's obvious admiration for it, would suffice to contradict us. This garden is the idyllic place for amorous encounters; Agnès Varda captures this aspect in her moving film, *Cléo de cinq à sept*, in which

The Parc Montsouris, a true English-style garden planted with remarkable trees, is organized in levels around the peaceful lake where ducks, swans and waterhens nest.

a young soldier mobilized for the Algerian War meets a mysterious woman waiting in anguish for the results of medical tests. And Jacques Prévert, in a wonderful poem in *Paroles*: "Thousands and thousands of years / Would not suffice / To describe / The little second in eternity / In which you kissed me / In which I kissed you / In Montsouris park in Paris / In Paris / On earth / Earth that is a star." The fact remains that Montsouris (not completed until 1878) does not measure up to the standards of the Buttes-Chaumont.

The virtuosity with which Alphand disguised the two railway lines that intersect at the park (the Petite Ceinture and the Sceaux line) is admirable; he transformed their trenches into ravines with mountain pastures and pine trees. Nevertheless, this clever solution did not reduce the overall uniformity of the park. Everything there is beautiful: the gently sloping lawns on which magpies, blackbirds, rooks and starlings frolic; the majesty of the lime tree, the great cedar tree, the Virginia tulip tree, the Judas tree, the Siberian elm, the *sempervirens* sequoia and the *Poncirus trifoliata*; the conservative yet picturesque brook, waterfall and lake with its swans, mallards, pochards and sheldrakes; the opulence of the azaleas, hostas, ferns and bergenias — beautiful, yes, but there are no surprises. Apart from the sensuality of the vegetation and the adventure of exploring the grottoes, there is little that reflects "all that is strange about a man" of which Aragon spoke when describing the Buttes-Chaumont.

Montsouris is as tidy and well groomed as a painting by Cabanel. There was even a colonial note provided by the scaled-down reproduction of the Bey's palace in Tunis, the Bardo, which unfortunately burned down in 1991 — it was one of the attractions of the 1867 Exposition. Faced with so much

perfection and cool beauty, it is difficult to imagine that bandits hid in the quarries in the area called "Mocquesouris."

Even harder to believe is the fiasco that surrounded the park's inauguration. The speeches for the important guests were well underway when a catastrophe occurred. The large lake that was the centerpiece of this first version of the park had just been filled, when it suddenly emptied again like a vulgar sink! Paris laughed, the emperor was furious, Alphand returned to the drawing board and, worst of all, the engineer responsible for the work committed suicide.

Up to his death in 1891, Alphand reigned supreme over the "embellishment" of Paris. However, after Montsouris was completed,

The tall black pines in Montsouris shelter the beautiful Fer à Cheval stairway (above). Beyond the monumental cedars stood the replica of the Bey of Tunis's palace, ravaged by fire in March 1991 (following page).

he concentrated on cleaning the city and modernizing its transport system, leaving the responsibility for his landscape work to Laforcade, André and Deny, with the collaboration of Davioud and later Formigé for the *fabriques*. He limited his gardening activities to maintaining the promenades that had already been laid out, to building squares — none of which achieved the "classic" perfection of the Square du Temple, the Tour Saint-Jacques (unfortunately disfigured by its restoration in 1968) or Batignolles — and to creating the major gardens of the Trocadéro and the Champ-de-Mars for the Universal Expositions.

The Trocadéro and the Champ-de-Mars, designed to hold temporary exhibitions, still exist. But time, fashion and the successive

exhibitions held there until just before the last war have altered them so much that they are no longer representative of Alphand's style. Geometry and perspective, in abeyance since the middle of the eighteenth century, have reconquered the space.

To discover what is in fact a single garden bisected perpendicularly by the Seine in the guise of a "grand canal," offering a vista of over one kilometer that runs from the École Militaire to the open esplanade of the Trocadéro, why not climb to the first level of the Eiffel Tower on a bright summer morning?

Above the river with its bustling barges, the air trembles in the heat. The sun, already high, bounces blindingly off the marble façades of the Palais de Chaillot. With its huge, rigid, concave wings and its grandiose bas-reliefs, the Speero-Mussolino-Stalinist monument is a reminder that, in 1937, the date of the last Parisian Universal Exposition and the eve of the Second World War, French democracy was shot through with the totalitarian visions that were leading Europe toward the apocalypse. But the wide neoclassical space between the symmetrical buildings, framed by sloping terraces and landscaped gardens, is handsomely noble. A succession of basins, reminiscent of those of Saint-Cloud or Marly, runs from the upper platform.

This ancient catalpa in the Parc Montsouris died in February 1990, toppled by the storm that destroyed hundreds of trees in Paris (top). This elegant Virginian tulip-tree is one of the numerous species in this park, including poplars, limes, Japanese maples and copper beeches (above). Beneath the foliage of the park runs a small river that can be crossed by jumping on the large stones (facing).

The extremely complicated hydraulic mechanism concealed in the hill which makes this marvel possible was the work of a team (Thiers, Maitre and Expert) headed by the landscapist and architect Jacques Gréber. Through his efforts Parisians can enjoy, especially during heat waves, a vast and majestic open-air water garden.

On the opposite bank of the Seine, at the foot of the Eiffel Tower where four pillars form a gigantic transparent vault, crowds of visitors cross the two landscaped gardens that offer ponds, rock grottoes, lawns, shrubbery, flower beds and avenues shaded by willow and cypress trees. A cosmopolitan, noisy, polyglot multitude pours ceaselessly out of the buses. What does this gregarious mass actually see? Few take the time to walk in the Champ-de-Mars, which is a pity. This site was the setting for celebrations organized by the painter David during the Revolution, especially those of July 14, 1790.

An immense green carpet unrolls into a lawn in front of the École Militaire, from which a young Corsican named Napoleon Bonaparte graduated as an artillery lieutenant in 1786. This vast rectangle (600 x 700 meters) consists of a series of contrasting gardens. Those near the Eiffel Tower are dense with winding paths, clumps of rhododendrons and

astonishings groups of trees that include maples, plane trees and limes, an occasional lacquer tree, *Eucommia ulmoïdes*, and *Alnus cordifolia*, or weeping ash. The untrammelled freedom of this area contrasts beautifully with the rigorous geometry of the central lawn bordered by cone-shaped yews. A circular mall surrounding an oblong basin in the center and planted with a ring of plane trees enclosing a second ring of soapberry trees, sets off the intersection of the avenue Suffren. It is followed by another group of flourishing gardens, complete with a kiosk, merry-go-rounds, children's games and a puppet theater. Finally, opposite the École Militaire, alternating rows of pruned soapberry trees end at an esplanade that has a fountain, stairs and a balustrade. A neoclassical structure links the elegant architecture of the École to the majestic gardens.

The eclecticism that rules this group of monuments is deliberate. But this kind of synthesis, however refined, betrays the hesitation of the designers faced with the crisis that began to affect Alphand's academicism. In fact, the development of "democratic" urban parks in America, a concept invented by Olmsted — who designed Central Park to attract crowds of New Yorkers in need of fresh air and greenery to this huge area in the heart of Manhattan — posed a new set of problems in the late nineteenth century. This novel approach, coupled with a return to a classic formalism and a fresh examination of the city, nature and light by the Impressionist and Symbolist painters, brought "Alphandism" under fire.

The result was a style called "mixed" or "composite" by one of its creators, Jules Vacherot, head gardener of Paris at the time of the World's Fair of 1900. His book, *Les Parcs et jardins au début du XXe siècle* (1908), dominated the public horticultural creations in Paris until the end of the 1930s. The style

The double row of plane trees underscores the sober lines and the far-reaching view of the Champ-de-Mars.

began as a combination of neoclassicism and landscape art, then some *japonisme* drawn from art nouveau was added in the 1890s, followed by a touch of cubism filtered through art deco after the First World War.

Paradoxically, this reversion to a form of classicism resulted from a rejection of Alphandism. Henri Duchêne was working in the Parisian urbanism department in the shadow of Alphand and Édouard André when, in 1877, he decided to break with his superiors and their dogmatism that had become so pervasive that even Versailles and the Tuileries were in danger of being "landscaped."

The Duchêne agency — for Henri was joined by his son Achille (1866-1945) — then chose to concentrate its efforts on the rehabilitation

of the "classical French style," drawing from the same inspiration as Puvis de Chavannes and the Parnassian poets. They were so successful that Achille, known to rich landowners throughout the world as the "Napoleon of gardening," went beyond the restoration of historical gardens inititated by his father. After rehabilitating Vaux-le-Vicomte, Champs-sur-Marne, Wideville, Courances, Le Marais, Breteuil, La Villette and even Blenheim in England (the work of the great English landscape artist Capability Brown!), each redesigned according to a neoclassical spirit that mixed modern materials and planting techniques with old geometric layouts, Achille Duchêne proceeded to design a great many private and public gardens in France and abroad. In the United States he worked for the millionaires Carolan and Belmont; in England he was praised to the

Secluded groves of trees and shrubs add a lovely charm to the Champ-de-Mars.

skies by the Duke of Marlborough; in Argentina he became extremely famous; while in Paris he designed the gardens of the Cambacérès and Matignon Hôtels. Achille Duchêne was less popular after the luxury of the prewar years disappeared and the idea of a "French good taste" faded, but he had by then earned a faithful following. During the 1930s, the landscapists Gréber, Otin, Duprât, Péanh, Laprade and Riousse, while each attempting to set a personal style, recognized their debt to both Duchêne and to the geometric style — in other words, the redefinition of Le Nôtre in contemporary terms.

Achille Duchêne's fame was so widespread that it was natural that Albert Kahn hired him as a consultant shortly after starting the gardens of the riverside property he purchased in Boulogne-Billancourt in 1893. But Kahn's mind was infinitely more inquiring, more open, more generous, more fanciful and more preoccupied with philosophical questions than was Duchêne's — in short, his humanism was radical and universal. Furthermore, his restless and contradictory personality was far removed from the uncomplicated equilibrium preached by the "Napoleon of gardening." More baroque than classical, Albert Kahn chose eclecticism not because he was unsure of his direction, like Vacherot, but from a conscious ethical belief. He wanted to display the best from each nation, the better to understand and assimilate it. Consequently Albert Kahn let Duchêne design only the rose garden and the French-style garden around the main greenhouse in the center of his property. He then designed the rest exactly as he pleased, despite his many collaborators and a plethora of Japanese gardeners. In a spirit resembling Segalen, Monet and Debussy, Kahn set about assembling the most unusual combinations of plants, expressive colors and delicate materials into a whole that followed the precepts of art nouveau, with curving and geometric shapes expressing symbolism, abstraction, *japonisme* and modernism.

Albert Kahn was not only self-taught, or rather, an amateur gardener, he was also an innovator who assimilated the ideas of the painters and thinkers of his time to a greater degree than did Duchêne. He would have been called the master of the Parisian horticultural art of the turn of the century had there not been an even greater "professional" figure standing in the shadows. This was Jean-Claude-Nicolas Forestier, as indispensable as he was unrecognized.

Like Barillet-Deschamps ("Fields") and Achille Duchêne ("Oak"), Jean-Claude-Nicolas Forestier (1861-1930) had a name that seemed to foretell his career. And yet it was with great reluctance that he decided to join the Department of Waterways and Forests when he left the École Polytechnique. Jean Giraudoux, who was the most illustrious of his friends after Claude Monet, sketched the portrait of an artist who was never given the opportunity to create a major work worthy of his talent in France, even though he was appointed curator of the western section of the Promenades de Paris in 1898: "Beloved by the ducks on the lake, the only Parisian from whom the does in the woods never fled, he contemplated Cologne with a sore heart; with an ironical smile, he left our strangling traffic to design open spaces in Brazil and to plant flowers in Florida. And the only satisfaction he received before he died was to plan the profusion of flowers that suddenly invaded the Luxembourg Gardens and the Champs-Élysées and to contribute to the rescue of the Parc de Sceaux, which is now one of the most beautiful and the largest garden in Paris" (*Pleins Pouvoirs*, 1947).

Although he designed many private gardens in Spain and in southern France (the Bastide du Roy near Biot for the Countess Polignac and

Spectacles of overwhelming beauty are created by the magic of water and light at Trocadéro (facing). The "Majesteuse" fountain at Trocadéro, as it is called by the gardeners, spews forth millions of liters of water, which are transformed into ephemeral mists and magical drops (following page).

the Jardin Joséph-Guy in Béziers), Forestier was first and foremost a gardener-cum-town planner. Pursuing the polemic raised by Olmsted in the United States, Forestier wrote *Grandes Villes et systèmes de parcs* (1906), an essay in which "nature," adapted as a garden in the modern city, is part of a hierarchic system that includes areas of pleasure and rest which allow nature to live and grow. But he never had the opportunity to carry out this program in Paris. Instead, through his connections with the family of the former Empress Eugénie, he went to Spain, where he was able to demonstrate his worth (as he was to do in Havana) by designing the Maria Luisa Park in Seville and the Montjuich Gardens in Barcelona. These gardens of exceptional intrinsic beauty became harmonious extensions of these cities during the International Expositions of 1911 and 1916.

Still, his work in Paris was hardly negligible: besides maintaining the existing woods and promenades, restoring the Parc de Sceaux, redesigning the Champs-Élysées, Champ-de-Mars and, above all, the Bagatelle, he created the Parc de la Cité Universitaire.

Both the choice of the site — opposite Montsouris — and the design of this urban park provide a reasonably precise idea of how Forestier might have developed Paris had he not been so shackled by administrative regulations. He was motivated by two main preoccupations: the aesthetic aspect of gardens and the future development of Paris.

His aesthetic concern led him to integrate contemporary ideas into his concept of gardening. He enriched his botanical palette, refreshing our Western culture by assimilating

At the top of Square Willette, the immaculately white Sacré-Coeur Basilica rises above a crown of trees. Built with stone from Château-Landon, the basilica turns even whiter when it rains.

"exotic" and "primitive" components, and he drew his ideas about color, form and light from modern painting and architecture. His extensive botanical knowledge made him a master in the handling of diverse plants, and his interest in the "archaic," in orientalism and especially in the Italian "pre-Raphaelite" gardens or the Moorish gardens of Andalusia (from which he borrowed compartmentalization and terraced designs), led to a friendship with Monet, whom he used to visit in his famous garden at Giverny. A mutual respect also developed between Forestier and Le Corbusier (whose *Pavilion de l'Esprit Nouveau* at the Exposition of Decorative Arts of 1925 he imposed and championed). Hence, too, the similarity of style between his drawings and those of Viennese *Secession* artists such as Franz Lebisch, Emil Hoppe and Max Benirschke.

The "line" is similar, as is the recourse to geometric compositions that were foreign to the neoclassical spirit. Forestier was much more influenced by the masters of art nouveau than was Achille Duchêne, although a few years later he became interested in the experiments of artists such as André Véra, Gabriel Guévrékian and Rob Mallet-Stevens, who were to complete the "denaturizing" of art nouveau by assimilating cubism and neoplasticism; in other words, they embraced an increasingly abstract geometric formalism.

The second of Forestier's obsessions concerned the future of Paris. How could he prevent the asphyxiation of a densely populated city surrounded by suburbs that, though less crowded, were expanding at an alarming rate? Whereas Haussmann had concentrated on the development of intramural Paris, Forestier's

The Square Willette, with its rigorous design, remarkable view and magnificent honey locust, orange, araucaria and magnolia trees is a lovely, sophisticated garden.

scope was much larger: he adopted the courageous policy taken by New York authorities toward Central Park, which encouraged the acquisition of vast real estate preserves protected from property speculation. These were to be reserved for the creation of parks and gardens that would be places of beauty and relaxation, while ensuring that there would always be the possibility of improving traffic flow and the city's internal network.

Among other projects, Forestier dreamed of linking Paris to the suburbs with a belt of gardens designed to occupy the former city walls. His hopes were dashed by developers, but he was, however, able to create the beautiful and strange garden city known as the Cité Universitaire in 1922 with the collaboration of Lucien Bechmann and Louis Azéma.

Here the *fabriques* consist of the student lodgings, groups of pavilions interlinked by a network of strictly designed gardens. The tenants of the boulevard Jourdan are to be envied, for in May and June the avenues flanked with colorful flower beds are a delight. Rambling roses perfume the "villages" of the French Provinces and the Deutsch-de-la-Meurthe Foundation, and bushes, trees and flowers bloom profusely in great colored masses. Yet the sobriety of the underlying geometric design becomes apparent near the Maison Internationale, where a series of planted areas and "cubist" flagging reaches the perron that leads to the university restaurant and theater. The park, which extends from the "Petite Ceinture" as far as the ring road, is laid out with the neatness of an American campus, and vast areas are left open for games and sports.

The dense "Queen Elizabeth" rose forms thick and velvety flower beds in the Parc de Choisy.

Forestier died in 1930, shortly before Le Corbusier formulated the principles of a new "rational" urbanism. This decisive, brilliant and dramatic turning point was to lead to a dictatorship of "open spaces." However, it was to be a long time before these revolutionary theories were put into practice, despite the Exposition of Decorative Arts of 1925, where Le Corbusier presented a roof garden, Guévrékian some triangular basins painted with bright colors by Robert Delaunay, and Mallet-Stevens a reinforced concrete "cubist tree." Paris therefore owes some of its more remarkable gardens to equally talented but more traditional landscape-architects of the 1930s.

The earliest of these, the Square Saint-Lambert, continues the tradition of the Alphandian square but renews its form.

Situated in the heart of what was still quite recently a popular district — the fifteenth arrondissement — the square was created in 1933 by the architect Georges Sébille on the site of the Vaugirard gasworks. He was able to make elegant use of the vat that once contained gas by transforming it into a circular basin in which, as soon as the weather turns warm, children paddle and splash. Opposite the basin near the large terrace are three forked paths that frame two geometric parterres; despite the somewhat restricted space, they provide a pleasant "French-style" view enhanced by farthingale borders. Young children run shrieking and tumbling across the lawn under the watchful eyes of their mothers; but on the terrace, designed in a landscapist style with cedrelas and pterocaryas from which hang long pale green catkins, adolescents dream of more dangerous games.

Between the well-designed curve of water spouts in the Parc de Choisy, the colors of the flowers change and multiply freely.

The Parc de Choisy, also on the left bank but in the thirteenth arrondissement, is another garden that reflects geometry and landscaping in a joyful image that contrasts with the ugliness of the high-rise apartments in what is now a Parisian Chinatown. Created in 1937 in an area twice the size of Square Saint-Lambert (ten acres instead of four) by the architect Édouard Crevel, this garden integrates the Medico-Dental Institute by using it as a château or large villa. The presence of the Institute determined the design of the garden. The main axis, at present spoiled by a handsome but overpowering sculpture by Richard Serra (whose removal, however, has been decreed), faces the building and is organized into a playground bordered by alternate rows of trees framing a pair of tranquil gardens sheltered by foliage. A subsidiary axis with a central "French-style" basin runs perpendicular to this. On either side of the building, dense landscapist-style gardens soften the Institute's architectural rigidity. In addition, the garden offers numerous activities (merry-go-round, theater, soda fountain, play area, sand pits, various games) and typical 1930s-style garden furniture. A round table in porphyry, a gift from Finland after the 1937 Universal Exposition, stands not far from the main building at the foot of three majestic ash trees.

The Palais de Chaillot, built for this last great prewar celebration on the site of the old Trocadéro, was the work of three somewhat uninspired architects. And yet one of these, Louis Azéma, designed the vast twelve-acre Square de la Butte-du-Chapeau-Rouge on the heights of the nineteenth arrondissement, near boulevard Serurier, considered to be a masterpiece of the 1930s. This praise is exaggerated; the term testimony would be more apt since this remote garden's charm stems primarily from its precipitate site, enhanced by magnificent hedges of clipped box-trees that stand one meter high. Like Chaillot, the rest of the Square de la Butte-du-Chapeau-Rouge — portico/terrace, staircases, red-brick shelters and fountains, glass paving and colored concrete — is overly theatrical and obviously the work of an architect rather than a landscaper. Yet the view from its promontories is superb: in the foreground lie the white terraces of the Robert Debré Hospital, conceived by its architect Pierre Riboulet as a great ship anchored at the flank of the Pré-Saint-Gervais hill. Behind it stands the tall gray mass of the Paris Archives building, created through the subtle genius of Henri Gaudin and his son Bruno, and all around, noisy with the traffic on the ring road, throbs the violent life of the city.

Returning to the right bank and the thirteenth arrondissement, the ring road leads to the largest garden of the period, Parc Kellermann — also the last to be begun (1939) — hidden in a natural hollow near the Peupliers postern. Finished in 1950, this pleasant arrangement in the "composite" style is the single major Parisian work by Jacques Gréber who, like Forestier, created his greatest works outside his own country (such as the famous Parkway in Philadephia). Set in what was once the bed of the Bièvre river, Parc Kellerman is a mixture of wide terraces, geometric staircases

Not far from the play area is the Group Dedicated to the Child, *a tender work by the sculptor Traverse (above).*

bordered with perfumed plants (broom, lavender), shrubs with flowers and berries such as arbutus, handsomely rounded lawns and a generous foliage of trees, mostly ash, willow and poplar (due to the damp soil). It is a pleasure, especially at the height of summer when the heat melts the asphalt in the *allées* leading to the Butte-aux-Cailles, to wander through this welcoming yet secretive garden. There is an unpretentious artistry in every detail, with just enough control over the vegetation so that it harmonizes with the irregularities of the terrain.

The Parisian masterpiece of the 1930s is not Parc Kellerman, however, but a nearby square that is, like the park, set in the bed of the Bièvre: Square René-Le Gall. Its oldest part, once called "Square des Gobelins," dates from 1938.

Surprisingly, the park lies below street level, for its elongated, nearly rectangular site was once an island in the center of the now underground river that joined the Seine near Austerlitz station. And since the jugglers of the Pont-Neuf habitually let their monkeys frisk about there, the island was nicknamed "monkey island." Later on, the Gobelins tapestry manufacturers used to treat the wool there along with tanners and washerwomen; other polluting crafts also used the area with the result that the Bièvre that Watteau found so refreshing became a sewer that had to be covered up. A square was then placed on "monkey island." In time it became so dilapidated and overgrown that during the rule of the Popular Front, Jean-Charles Moreux (1889-1956) was commissioned to redesign it.

The Square de Butte-du-Chapeau-Rouge is beautiful even in winter, when the typical 1930s style is evident (top). In Square René Le Gall, the 1930s stairway descends to a rustic thicket in which all the bucolic varieties of plants in the Île de France flourish (following page).

Moreux had been a member of the avant-garde during the 1920s. With Paul Véra and Gabriel Guévrékian he participated in the invention of a landscape "cubism," best represented by the garden of Charles de Noailles's *hôtel* that faced the Place des États-Unis. Unfortunately, it no longer exists, but Man Ray's photographs reveal its design. It covered five hundred square meters; vertical mirrors set at intervals around the edges of the garden, and geometric marquetry, alternating with flagging and colored gravel linked by triangles of plants and rare flowers, created chromatic reflections in the style of a Braque still life, with colors worthy of Delaunay. But by 1938 Moreux had finished with this kind of experiment, although he still preferred a geometric rather than a romantic landscape.

His first step in Square Gobelins was to link rue Croulebarbe and rue Berbier-du-Mets to the "island" below them with superb stairways. On the garden side they are covered with a pattern of flint buried in the concrete, and lower planks each hold a huge cement ball. This design, with the high walls that surround the garden and the severe Conservatoire du Mobilier National that overlooks it, accentuates the nature of the site. It is a long boxed-in parallelepiped that must be admired from above before entering it from below.

The northern part of the garden makes countless allusions to the Renaissance. Its supporting walls are decorated with rockwork by Maurice Garnier that mixes pebbles and shells, which in a "surrealist" tone similar to Arcimboldo's figures evoke the masks of the Tivoli. The style of the first section of the garden, situated on an esplanade along the axis of the stairs, is clearly inspired by Villandry. Four bowers covered in climbing roses surround yews cut in arabesques that in turn encircle a rustic obelisk. It is reminiscent of the sublime gardens on the banks of the river Cher, restored by Moreux during the same period, after the engravings by Androuet du Cerceau.

Facing this neat wood, a straight avenue enters a grove full of the more common species of trees that make it resemble the forests of Île-de-France. And if the beeches, ash, wild cherry trees, yoke elms, lime trees, walnut trees, birches, maples, hawthorns and bluish poplars lining the north wall grow so beautifully, it is because the humidity rising from the ancient bed of the Bièvre makes them glow with health.

The third and last part of the garden, a playground bordered by two stoa-shaped porticoes that serve as a courtyard, is contrastingly open and sunny. Unfortunately it is encumbered by slides, ladders and other such equipment; their standardized mediocrity provides a sad counterpoint to the refinement of Moreux's work.

A secret, precious and subtle garden. A learned garden that mixes nature and culture, history and virgin woods, light and shadow, vegetation and minerals. Once discovered, Square René Le Gall can never be forgotten, in spite of its small size, for art has always had the power to bewitch the mind.

*An obelisk gives the Square René Le Gall
a vaguely Renaissance atmosphere (above). In the style of
Arcimboldo, rocks, pebbles, shells and fossils form the
unusual decoration of the staircase in the square (facing). Light plays
on the basin in the Parc Georges Brassens (following page).*

9

CONTEMPORARY
GARDENS

The art of gardening, usually linked to decorative or utilitarian purposes, even today often produces floral or hygienic creations that are measured only in the number of turfed acres, trees or square meters of flower beds.

"We protect thousands of acres of public parks"; "We have created more parks and gardens in ten years than in the previous century"; "We have planted 500,000 rose-bushes in ten years," announced posters in Paris in 1990 featuring green lawns or a block of roses compressed by the sculptor César. This is both encouraging and disturbing. Those who love greenery and roses cannot but applaud the attempt to give every Parisian a "garden" within six hundred meters of his home, and soon, planted "promenades," but the fact remains that an essential element is missing from these proclamations. Gardens can no more be evaluated in quantitative terms than music by the amount of notes, literature the volume of words or painting the number of colors. As in any art form, it is only after the technical considerations have been taken care of that the true art emerges.

Although even the smallest patch of greenery can improve an unattractive urban view, just as a climbing vine can make the dullest wall delightful, it has nevertheless become essential — at a time when there is a renewal in garden design — to break with the old policy of reducing a city garden to a "green space."

On the south bank of the Seine, the Tino Rossi Garden created in 1977 is a measure of the crisis that has afflicted the art of gardening developed by Le Nôtre and Barillet-

The Tino Rossi Garden, an open-air museum of contemporary sculpture, is reflected in the water of the Seine (above). Trellises, arcades, bowers and arbors covered with honeysuckle, jasmine and wisteria contribute to the charm of the garden at Les Halles (facing).

an aromatic garden planted with eighty
fragrant species; a rose garden; a stream;
a cool, damp garden full of arrowhead,
bulrushes and water lilies; a beehive;
a *pinot noir* vine in memory of the Morillon
and Périchot vintages that gave their name
to two neighboring streets; a garden of
heather, rhododendrons and azaleas;
a recreation area with a climbing wall and
play equipment; and an avenue of lime trees.
This park was created with the best
of intentions and was provided with a variety
of plants to create an attractive, relaxing area.
It is a pleasure to visit and to lie on the grass
in the summer, and the locals are truly
delighted with it. But a real garden lover
cannot but recognize that it is a succession
of more or less nostalgic anecdotes rather
than a modern evocation of nature within
a contemporary city.

Finally, the Parc de Belleville lies in a
symmetrical position in relation to Parc
Georges Brassens on an exceptional site in
northeast Paris. It is the geography of the
site itself rather than its environment, one of
the last remaining popular districts in Paris,
that makes this park interesting. The
upper promontory on the corner of rue Piat
and rue Envierges is one of the highest points
in the city. Although the view is no longer
the one that Quasimodo admired from the

towers of Notre Dame, the park offers a
magnificent perspective of roofs bristling with
towers, domes and belfries. The park area
itself descends toward Belleville and
Ménilmontant boulevards down an abrupt
slope that drops twenty-five meters.
The breadth of the landscape, underscored
as in Buttes-Chaumont by a gypsum quarry,
provided a perfect opportunity to bring the
picturesque style up to date. The park's
designer attempted to accomplish this by
visualizing a wild nature reinvading the
large gash made in the city's flank. Although
the use of the different levels and sheer slope
for the avenues was a good idea, the overall
quality of the work, which took twenty years
to complete, is disappointing. The garden
could have evoked the wastelands of Paris's
fortifications; instead there are wide paved
avenues framing lawns bordered in
conventional flower beds. The standard
lamp-posts, railings, orangery and
greenhouse mimic the past, and a cement rock
masquerading as a chalky outcrop looms
ponderously over the area. Perhaps our
modern technicians have forgotten the wisdom
of their predecessors who, despite more
primitive techniques, raised airy cement
mountains in the Buttes-Chaumont and
Vincennes Zoo that harmonized with the
trees and the overall urban landscape. Still,
the vegetation in Parc de Belleville is
finally hitting its stride, and if it grows as
profusely elsewhere as it does on the
trellises of the covered walk, this park just
might acquire a personality and a charm
of its own, provided it is allowed the
freedom to do so.

These creations of the 1970s were the
outcome of an odd deviation in garden
theory that began over twenty years earlier.
In Jacques Tati's *Mon oncle* (1957),
the family dances a lunatic ballet across the
lawn on arbitrarily laid out stepping stones.
In addition to being funny, that scene was

*The river runs from shallow ponds to cascades and
continues beneath the pines in the Parc Georges Brassens before
skirting the irises, ferns and variegated-leaf hostas.*

Early on, Jacques Simon, one of the major artisans of the renaissance of landscape theory, denounced this situation. Landscape architect Alain Richert believed that it was the result of a mutual ignorance of developments by the more adventurous innovators in landscape art and modern architecture. His well-informed and interesting theory merits a description.

According to Simon, when the English landscapist William Robinson created his "Wild Garden" in 1870, he rehabilitated wild plants which, by underscoring the existing character of the site through analogies of habitat, could create tensions so strong that their mere presence would replace the will of a designer. He thus invented a horticultural Impressionism, exploded traditional vistas and anticipated Land Art. But the majority of his successors misused his innovation in the manner of landscape designer Gertrude Jekyll: they planted the fashionable mixed borders described by Richert: "Cut a rectangular strip three centimeters wide by thirty centimeters high from a canvas by Monet; enlarge it a hundred times, lay it on the ground and you have a life-sized blueprint of a G. Jekyll mixed border, complete with color." Modern architects responded to this unstructured approach to planting

brilliantly observant: it mocked the loss of the sense of form that had characterized the architecture and landscape art of the postwar era.

There was no theory behind the layout, the relief of the terrain or the association of plants. This resulted in areas like the Parc Floral, the landscaped park in La Courneuve, and to a certain extent the departmental park in Nanterre, where an accumulation of undulating hillocks, meaninglessly shaped avenues, ponds and feats of gardening have no other object than to flatter the public's taste for flowers. Taken to an extreme limit, this pseudo-style implies the destruction of the garden in favor of that grassy residue of urban planning, the green space.

Built on the old embankment of the Couronnes, the Parc de Belleville is designed with terraces and slopes, and is dominated by a belvedere. An extraordinary play village was built for children, while a romantic stairway leads toward Paris beneath the blooming trellises.

series of previously established rules: these are the "points." Higher up, three registers of "lines" are superimposed: first, two perpendicular galleries are covered by an undulating metal porch roof designed by the Irish engineer Peter Rice, a master of high tech and the creator of the "cloud" at the Arche de la Défense. A weaving path then links the different sections of the park through "sequential" gardens that are pieced together like a film montage, and finally, tree-lined avenues lead to the main activities of the park. A set of "surfaces" completes the design; these are textured according to function (grass for recreation, flags or paving for entertainment areas), and the whole is brought to life by cafés and restaurants that stay open at night. A lighting system is planned, complete with spots and neon lights, to illuminate the avenues and galleries.

Bernard Tschumi won the New York *Progressive Architecture* magazine's 1985 prize for his design of the Parc de la Villette. The park has engendered numerous comments and articles all over the world. Now that the excitement has died down, this "deconstructivist" creation can now be appreciated for what it was intended to be: a sixty-two-acre public park.

The park's supporters underline the schism that it creates in the history of architecture and the art of gardening. Tschumi's conceptualism supposedly reflects our era, in which, according to Jean Baudrillard and Paul Virilio, the tangible will make way for immaterial networks of images and information. The relative lack of comprehension on the part of the public is therefore due to misunderstanding and

The collection of gardens at La Villette,
a twenty-first-century park, admirably unites architecture and
vegetation. In this space ruled by a conceptual design,
the audacity of the lines and forms can often surprise the stroller (above).
This is one of the follies of the park, a concrete
structure covered with painted sheet-metal (facing).

with running water that creates a microclimate, it is already possible to imagine the marvel it will become in a few years' time. The six species of dwarf, small and standard bamboo, and the seven species of rare bamboo will, when seen from the upper walk, form a light swell crossed with silver flashes. Below, after passing the "sound cylinder" by architect and musician Bernhard Leitner, the severe black-and-white stripes of a pebble paving by Daniel Buren leads to a warm, vibrant and reassuring world. According to Chemetoff, "The hollow here is not dissimulation but multiplication: a multiplication of atmospheres, of views, of patches of rediscovered sky. It is also silence, warmth, a climate adapted to the growth of plants, to contemplation and perhaps even to reflection. It is a chance for the visitor to notice unimportant things like the difference between *Phylostachis flexuosa* and *Pleiobastus linearis*, the difference in size between pebbles from the Drôme and bits of crushed basalt from the Ardèche." But the art of the garden, he continues, "is also a way of raising the question of modernity, not the modernity of objects and surfaces, but that of the land, its history and its richness — a stone in the garden of appearances."

Although the garden was planted as recently as 1987, its magic atmosphere reminiscent of one of Anduze's bamboo groves, the lighting equipment and furnishings have been carefully designed to create an atmosphere overflowing with a musical silence.

Because of the excessive beauty of the site, we have perhaps become too demanding. The Trellis Garden that follows the Bamboo Garden along the "cinematographic promenade" fails to provide the same enchantment. This creation by landscapists Gilles Vexlard and Laurence Vacherot, aided by the plastics technician Jean-Max Albert, is certainly not disagreeable, even though the

preconceptions: a prisoner of habit, the public naturally finds it hard to accept that an avant-garde artist could reveal the face of the future. Furthermore, the man in the street is unable to realize that a "totally modern" park should have the same relationship to a traditional country walk as electro-acoustic music has to the *Pastoral Symphony*. Nevertheless, there are many critics who do not agree with this denunciation of the "conservative" by the "avant-garde," and who feel that the intellectual and financial expenditure is out of proportion with the results, which could be qualified as banal.

At the moment, however, Alexandre Chemetoff's "Bamboo Garden" alone justifies a prolonged visit. Boxed into an artificial fault

A staircase leads to the Bamboo Garden behind the "sound cylinder" by Bernhard Leitner (above). Farther on, a forest of bamboos pushes toward the sky, their roots set in an artificial fault fed by a trickle of water (facing).

vegetation was planted only several years ago. Although the design of raised and compartmentalized tiers full of pansies is well thought out, and it will probably be pleasant to rest in the shade of the arbors in the warm weather, the area is less unusual than the Bamboo Garden. The materials are more conventional and the site more uniform, which means that it offers more limited perspectives. As for the third garden, which is visible, but not yet open to the public: it would be premature to speak about it at this point. Its designer Alain Pélissier saw it as radically "conceptual," but in its present state the plantless "water garden" is perplexing: what is the meaning of those small basins surrounded by colored bitumen? Without the ornamental fountains that present "water in all its guises," according to a computer program based on musical performances

(Henri Pousseur) or literature (Michel Butor), it is impossible to know.

From the beginning the promoters of this "major project," placed under the authority of the president of France, held tremendous ambitions for the Parc de la Villette. The park is intended to set an international standard for public parks of the late twentieth century; in other words, to be what Buttes-Chaumont or Central Park were to the nineteenth century. It is to be so far ahead of its time that the theory of landscape art for the third millenium will have already been formulated. Will the site's abstract scale and the sophisticated dialogue that replaces a plastic and vegetable complexity attain this goal? It is too soon to judge. Nevertheless, despite a number of scholarly excesses, this ambition is already having a positive effect. Thanks to the

The Arsenal basin at the Bastille is a small harbor with the charm of Saint-Tropez, surrounded by a pleasantly terraced garden.

worldwide debate that has arisen over Tschumi's work, interest in the art of gardening has increased. The number of books and articles have multiplied, and never in the last hundred years have so many new, high-quality projects been undertaken in Paris.

The known formulæ have been rejected. The updated Alphandism of the Parc de Belleville and the Parc Georges Brassens has not spread beyond the banks of the Arsenal Basin. And the Parc Citroën taking shape near Javel metro station has escaped the "Grands Prix de Rome" winners who would have made it into an extension of the so-called "contemporary" Front de Seine.

The promoters of the Parc Citröen, which is part of a major property development program, did not want to entrust the entire project to architect Patrick Berger and landscapist Gilles Clément. In an attempt to innovate cautiously, they searched for a compromise between the two ambitious young creators and a team with an established reputation, the architects Jodry and Viguier and the landscapist Alain Provost (who is a reputed professional, although his major work — the landscape park of La Courneuve — is a prime example of a 1960s-style "green space").

Despite the promoters' ambivalence and the considerable problems posed by this thirty-five-acre site — it faces the Seine but is surrounded by a rather inelegant architectural complex — Gilles Clément appears to have imposed his style. His success was so great that the question today is not whether there is a lack of intellectual purpose in the composition of the park; it may, in fact, have an excess of esoteric refinement.

Everything is symbolic in this vast park, which is scheduled to open in 1992. The central area consists of a long green lawn that leads from the two greenhouses on the city side to the edge of the river, which is dominated by the new viaduct for the RER railway. This great lawn set perpendicularly to the Seine will be dotted with lamp-posts that will light up according to formulæ that refer to the atomic numbers of metals. This order, based on the alchemist goal of transforming a base material (lead) into a noble one (gold), will also dictate the layout of the park, which is to represent the progress of Nature (the river) toward Artifice (the city) through the successive stages of Movement (or Metamorphosis) and Architecture.

On the left side facing the capital is the most "natural" of these gardens. It is called Movement, and will be filled with delicate wild plants. This garden will be followed by a series of seven "serial gardens," each with its own greenhouse; they will be separated from one another by a stream of water that flows toward the central lawn. These areas suggest the transmutation of lead into gold, an effect attained through a meticulous selection of rare plants resulting in gardens that are in turn gray, green, orange, red, silver, and golden. The final element will be a masterpiece of "artifice": a peristyle made of verdure and a white garden that, like white light, is a blend of every color in the spectrum.

The Parc André Citroën, now under construction, will consist of several gardens. The White Garden, in juxtaposition with the Black Garden, contains white-colored mineral and plant elements only.

expected of a garden." Three sequences framed by trees will run from west to east.

Open to the city, though cut off on the west by the trees around the Bercy Stadium, the Prairie will be a vast recreational area delineated by nine kiosks at the centers of the squares of the superimposed grid. This Prairie, bordering on its north side the new American Center designed by the Californian architect Frank Gehry, will be itself connected to the main terrace that separates — through the use of grass terraces edged with basins — the park from the motorway along the banks of the Seine.

Eight garden areas framing the central "archeological garden" will follow these shady seven-acre lawns: four "specific gardens"

comprising a market garden, an orchard, a rose garden and a garden of aromatic plants; and four "pavilion gardens" illustrating the seasons. These will include Winter, air, and the color white, indicated by the Tower of the Winds kiosk in the north; Summer, earth, and the color black, symbolized by a cube buried in polished granite set with golden nuggets in the south; Autumn, fire, and the color red, suggested by a chimney half-buried among vines in the west; and Spring, water, wind with a hollow cylinder and a round pond, suggesting a sanctuary in the east.

Although the design revolves around a grid, the last third of the park at the eastern edge is the "romantic" section, because the picturesque components are linked to the theme of water. A canal will join the two sides of the garden across rue de Dijon through a hypostyle grotto buried in a hill supporting the causeway; a square island will sit in the middle of a round basin fed by the canal; a waterfall will lead to another grotto at the end of the garden toward cours Chamonard; and there will be a flowering amphitheater, a belvedere and a tumulus decorated with an aviary.

This somewhat disinherited eastern sector of Paris is being transformed into a lively district and, like the western one, it will soon have a thoroughly modern park. The civil servants from the Ministry of Finance will share it with the children from the local apartment blocks, and students of this new "Latin Quarter" will cross the footbridge linking the Bibliothèque de France to the terrace of the Prairie. Winter will cover the lawns in snow, but in spring the old trees will burst into life. And, for the informed visitor, it will be a joy to wander through a park that combines beautiful foliage with a richly conceived design. Every step will confirm that the park's form and vegetation are in harmony and fulfill the demanding conditions for a complete art.

On the square in front of the Bercy Stadium, the Canyoneaustrate *is a concrete sculpture, a canyon landscape and a gigantic fountain (above). These old barrels evoke the memory of the former wine merchants who worked here; the area is now being redesigned as a huge park (facing).*

GARDEN GUIDE

This section lists by arrondissement the most interesting parks, gardens and squares in Paris; several exceptional ones on the outskirts of the capital are also noted. It is impossible to include all the sites in Paris — there are several hundred — but we have indicated the opening hours, address and a short description of parks that have the most spectacular trees, flowers and statues. The opening hours for squares vary with the seasons; however, they are generally open from 8 a.m. to sunset. Information concerning the opening days and hours of gardens that are part of museums can be obtained by calling the telephone number given for the museum.

Living near nature is possible in Paris and this guide lists the multiple pleasures to be enjoyed: sports, classes and leisure activities. For more information concerning the concerts performed in the bandstands, telephone 40.71.74.08 in Paris. Note also that it is not always forbidden to sit and rest on the grass — lawns are off-limits only once every three years, to allow the grass to regenerate.

Finally, if you would like more detailed information, refer to the list of guide books (p. 293) and guided tours (p. 291).

TUILERIES GARDENS
1564

Address - main entrance: Place de la Concorde - 75001 Paris - tel: 42.60.27.67.
Opening hours: Monday to Friday 7 a.m. (7:30 a.m. Saturdays, Sundays and holidays) to 8 p.m. (in winter) or 10 p.m. (in summer).

WHAT TO SEE: As the Tuileries are currently being restored, the greatest charm of this garden lies, for the moment, in the statues, particularly those from the former château at Marly and the magnificent Maillol bronzes. The work is scheduled to be completed in 1992.
ACTIVITIES: For children: pony rides, swings, model sailboat and cart rentals, play area. For adults: bowls.
RESTAURANTS: Four snack bars sell sandwiches and drinks; two of them serve light meals at tables under the trees.

PALAIS-ROYAL GARDEN
1629

Address: Place du Palais-Royal - 75001 Paris - tel: 42.60.16.87.
Opening hours: Daily 7 or 7:30 a.m. to 8:30, 9:30, 10 or 11 p.m., depending on the season.

WHAT TO SEE: Stroll along the elegant boutiques under the arcades and view the surprising black- and white-striped columns by Daniel Buren.
ACTIVITIES: Play areas.
RESTAURANTS: *La Gaudriole*, 30 rue Montpensier, tel: 42.97.55.49. In good weather, lunch and dinner are served on the terrace under the trees. *Muscade*, 36, rue Montpensier, tel: 42.97.51.36. Lunch and dinner on the terrace; tea salon open all day.

LES HALLES GARDEN
1983

Address: Forum des Halles - 75001 Paris - tel: 45.08.07.18 for the children's garden.
Opening hours: The garden for young children (entrance fee) is open Tuesdays through Sundays (closed Mondays).

WHAT TO SEE: The fountains and the waterways; the optic fiber sun dial, the tropical greenhouse, the multiple arbors, arcades and trellises.
ACTIVITIES: Two gardens, guarded by the topiary animals created by Claude Lalane, are reserved for children. The garden for children under the age of seven is guarded by topiary elephants. The largest garden (for seven- to eleven-year olds) is guarded by topiary rhinoceroses (free entrance). A merry-go-round and small antique train complete this interesting complex.
RESTAURANTS: There are many cafés and restaurants all around the garden in the Forum des Halles.

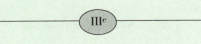

CARNAVALET MUSEUM GARDEN

Address: 23, rue de Sévigné - 75003 Paris - tel: 42.72.21.13.

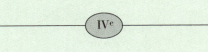

PLACE DES VOSGES
ca. 1388. Transformed into a square in 1866.

WHAT TO SEE: The magnificent arcades around the square; the garden is extremely beautiful at night when the recently restored fountains are illuminated.
RESTAURANTS: The many cafés under the arcades are good places from which to admire the garden.

THE HOTEL DE SENS
MUSEUM GARDEN

Address: Rue des Nonnains-d'Hyères - 75004 Paris - tel: 42.78.14.60.

THE HOTEL DE SULLY
MUSEUM GARDEN

Address: 48, rue Saint-Antoine - 75004 Paris - tel: 42.78.49.32.

SQUARE JEAN-XXIII
1844

This garden, which runs along the bank of the Seine at the base of Notre-Dame, was the first public garden in Paris.

JARDIN DES PLANTES
1576. Opened in 1640.

Address - main entrance: 57, rue Cuvier - 75005 Paris - tel: 40.79.30.00.
Opening hours: All year round, every day 9 a.m. to sunset. Alpine garden: April to September, 8:30 a.m. to 11 a.m., 1:30 p.m. to 5 p.m.; closed Tuesdays, Saturdays, Sundays and holidays. Winter garden (tropical greenhouses): 1 p.m. to 5 p.m.; closed Tuesdays and holidays. Zoo: 9 a.m. to 5 p.m. (in winter), 9 a.m. to 6 p.m. (in summer).

WHAT TO SEE: This garden has an exceptional collection of historic trees: Jussieu cedar, ginkgo biloba, Judas trees, Oriental plane trees, maple trees, Persian parrotias that turn bright red and gold in autumn. There is also an alpine garden, an iris garden, a rose garden, exceptional greenhouses, a zoo (entrance fee), a vivarium, and the "gloriette de Buffon." Guided visits to the Jardin des Plantes are available for groups of at least twenty people (reservations required).
ACTIVITIES: Discover the bird inhabitants of the garden with the "Wednesdays at the Museum" program at 9:15 a.m. An introductory course to the natural sciences is given at 2:30 p.m. Card and chess players meet under the *verrière* near rue Cuvier; there is a play area for children and bowls for adults.
RESTAURANTS: Light meals are served inside the zoo enclosure (currently under restoration). Near the iris garden, from April to October, the *Oasis* places tables under the row of plane trees. Several snack bars sell drinks, candy and toys.

ARÈNES DE LUTÈCE
1890

Address: 49-51, rue Monge - 75005 Paris - tel: 46.34.65.18.
Opening hours: Daily 10 a.m. to 7 p.m.

WHAT TO SEE: The arena dates from ancient Gaul. There are stones from Gallo-Romain ruins; rare trees, including a twisted beech tree and an olive tree in the square Capitan below.
ACTIVITIES: For children: a sports area and a play area. For adults: bowls, concerts and, occasionally, performances in the theater.

MOSQUE GARDEN
1920

Address: 2, place du Puits-de-l'Hermite - 75005 Paris - tel: 45.35.97.33. Opening hours: 9:30 a.m. to noon, 2 p.m. to 6:30 p.m.; closed Fridays.

WHAT TO SEE: The Hispano-Moorish patio of the mosque, and the garden. Visits are conducted by a guide (entrance fee).
RESTAURANTS: The mosque serves delicious mint tea; open 11 a.m. to 8 p.m.

TINO-ROSSI GARDEN
1977

Address: Quai Saint-Bernard - 75005 Paris.

WHAT TO SEE: The garden, embellished with curves and volumes, contains lavender, rosemary and thousands of seasonal plants that are changed from spring to autumn; the open-air sculpture museum includes work by Nicolas Schöffer, Ipoustéguy, César, Brancusi, Stahly, Zadkine.
ACTIVITIES: Play area for children, skating area.

SQUARE VIVIANI
1928

This charming square, near the oldest church in Paris (Saint Julien-le-Pauvre, fourth century), offers a lovely view of Notre-Dame. It has the oldest tree in the capital, a 380-year-old locust tree.

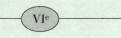

SQUARE LAURENT-PRACHE
1909

Address: Place Saint-Germain-des-Prés - 75006 Paris.

WHAT TO SEE: A bronze head of a woman (1950) by Picasso, sculpted as a tribute to Guillaume Apollinaire.

LUXEMBOURG GARDENS
1615

Address: 15, rue de Vaugirard or boulevard Saint-Michel - 75006 Paris -

tel: 42.34.20.23 or offices of the Senate fiscal department, tel: 42.34.20.23. Opening hours: 7:30 or 8:15 a.m. (depending on the season) to between 4:30 p.m. and 9:30 p.m. In case of snow, the gates are opened only after all the *allées* have been cleared by the gardeners.

WHAT TO SEE: The recently restored apiary; the Medici fountain, the "mushroom" kiosks for the guards; a collection of beautiful trees: Siberian elm, Virginia tulip tree, Chinese soapberry. The orchards, visible from the *allées*, can be visited only during tours organized the first Wednesday of the month (meet at 10 a.m. at the Pavillon de la Pépinière, 55 bis, rue d'Assas). The orangery hosts a series of exhibitions from May to October that generally concern gardening: mushrooms, exotic fruits, and so on.
ACTIVITIES: This is a children's paradise with a merry-go-round (complete with rings), pony rides, swings, a toy and candy kiosk, small carts, a puppet theater (tel: 43.29.50.97), and model-boat rental. For adults: tennis, basketball, bowls, chess, free concerts starting in the spring in the bandstands (the program is posted on the bandstand).
RESTAURANTS: The *Vialla Café* (between the Medici fountain and the grand basin) serves a light lunch on tables under the trees; snacks and waffles are available near the puppet theater; close to a dozen snack bars sell fruit juices and mineral water.
INSTRUCTION: Practical classes in fruit growing (open to the public) are given by the Luxembourg Horticultural School. For information, call: 42.34.23.62.
Bee-keeping classes are given at the apiary by the Apiculture Association. For information, call: 45.42.29.08.

SQUARE FÉLIX-DESRUELLES
1872

Address: 168 bis, boulevard Saint-Germain - 75006 Paris.

WHAT TO SEE: The monumental ceramic stoneware portal from Sèvres and art nouveau decor by Jules Coutan.

INSTITUT CATHOLIQUE GARDEN
1613

Address: 21, rue d'Assas - 75006 Paris.

For guided tours of the building and garden, contact Father Dupuy, tel: 45.48.05.16.

WHAT TO SEE: The garden of the main courtyard and the beautiful private garden.

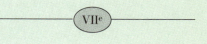

CHAMP-DE-MARS GARDEN
1778. Modified in 1927.

WHAT TO SEE: This garden extends to directly under the Eiffel Tower. There are beautiful trees: Himalayan abelia, cedar and wide-topped pterocarya.
ACTIVITIES: For children: puppet theater, pony rides and cart rental, swings, merry-go-round, play areas, a sports field (handball, volleyball, basketball), skating area. For adults: bowls. Concerts are given in the bandstand in the summer.
RESTAURANTS: Several snack bars sell drinks and waffles.

BABYLONE GARDEN
1978

Address: 31, rue de Babylone - 75007 Paris.

WHAT TO SEE: The vineyard and the apple orchard. This surprising garden has a provincial charm.
ACTIVITIES: Play area for children.

PARC DES MISSIONS-ÉTRANGÈRES
1663

Address: 128, rue du Bac - 75007 Paris - tel: 45.48.19.92.

WHAT TO SEE: This is a splendid, secluded garden planted with peach, chestnut and lime trees, and remarkable cedars. To visit the garden, write to the director of the Missions Étrangères.

RODIN MUSEUM GARDEN

Address: 77, rue de Varenne - 75007 Paris - tel: 47.05.01.34.

RESTAURANT: The cafeteria in the middle of the garden is a delightful place for a light lunch (tel: 45.56.16.97).

INTENDANT GARDEN
1980

Address: Avenue de Tourville -
75007 Paris.

WHAT TO SEE: An ornamental pool in
the center of a French-style garden
surrounded by clipped yew trees. Don't
miss the Jardin de l'Abondance on the
other side of the Saint-Louis-des-
Invalides Church.

PARC MONCEAU
1851

Address: Boulevard de Courcelles -
75008 Paris - tel: 40.53.00.15.
Opening hours: 8 a.m. to 7 p.m. (in
winter), 8 a.m. to 9:30 or 10 p.m. (in
summer).

WHAT TO SEE: The Chartres Rotunda by
Ledoux, the Naumachia, a Renaissance
arcade, the Carmontelle Pyramid, the
beautiful gates by Davioud. Remarkable
trees in the park include a sycamore
maple (the largest tree in Paris), figs,
plane trees, a superb copper beech.
Nineteenth-century sculptures include
portraits of Chopin, Maupassant,
Gounod, Musset.
ACTIVITIES: For children: play area,
merry-go-round, swings, skating area.
RESTAURANTS: A snack bar sells drinks
and waffles.

BOIS DE VINCENNES
1860

Address: Avenue Daumesnil or avenue
de Gravelle - 75012 Paris -
tel: 43.74.60.49.
Opening hours: The Georges-Ville farm
is open to the public Saturdays, Sundays
and holidays 10 a.m. to 5 or 7 p.m.,
depending on the season (tel:
43.28.47.63).

WHAT TO SEE: The zoo (tel:
43.43.84.95); three lakes: the Lac
Daumesnil and Lac des Minimes are
especially romantic; the unusual
architecture of the International
Buddhist Institute built for the

Colonial Exhibition of 1937; the pagoda,
occasionally open to the public (tel:
43.41.86.48); the Chinese pagoda at the
entrance to the Tropical and
Agronomical Research Institute; the
Belvedere; beautiful trees, including
plane trees, American black walnuts,
rowans, cedars, wild cherry trees.
ACTIVITIES: Excursions on foot,
horseback and bicycle (rental available);
26 kilometers of footpaths; fishing and
boating on Lac Daumesnil and Lac des
Minimes; bowls; miniature golf on
Reuilly Island; the Foire de Trône in
April and May on the lawns of Reuilly;
the Georges-Ville farm (route de
Pesage), where you can discover a
traditional farm (stables, orchard,
vegetable garden, harvests).
RESTAURANTS: *Le Chalet des Îles* (tel:
43.07.77.07) is a pleasant place to dine
in the middle of a garden filled with
flowers. *Le Chalet de la Porte Jaune* (tel:
43.28.80.11) is wonderful for breakfast;
after entering through a rather
unattractive door, there is a small terrace
hidden under the trees near the lake.
Le Plateau de Gravelle (tel:
43.96.99.55) has a terrace in the middle
of a garden with trees and fountains.

PARC FLORAL
1969

Address: Entrance at the corner of the
route des Pyramides and the avenue des
Minimes. Bois de Vincennes -
75012 Paris - tel: 43.43.92.95
or Minitel 36.15 code "Parc Floral."
Opening hours: 9:30 a.m. to 5, 6, or
8 p.m., depending on the season
(entrance fee).

WHAT TO SEE: The Stahly fountain;
sculptures by Calder, Agam, Schöffer,
Van Thienen; the Four Seasons garden;
the valley of flowers; the pine forest and
fern collections; the dahlia garden; the
aquatic plant garden with lotus and
water lilies; the butterfly garden with a
surprising collection of butterflies from
Île-de-France (June to October); the iris
garden.
ACTIVITIES: A small train runs around
the park. For children: an immense play
area, well equipped with merry-go-
rounds, climbing toys, ping-pong, cart
rental and a theater for three- to eight-
year-olds (tel: 42.41.88.33). For adults:
miniature golf, quadricycles for rent,
various games in pavilion no. 12
(checkers, chess, billiards); *thé dansant*
May 1 and every Sunday 2:30 p.m. to
6:30 p.m. (on patio no. 10).

RESTAURANTS: There is a picnic area
under the trees near the children's play
area. Two cafés: *Le Bousquet* (tel:
43.98.28.78) and *Rose Citron* (tel:
48.08.33.88) serve light meals in the
garden. The restaurant *La Chesnale du
Roy* (tel: 43.74.67.50) has a terrace
overlooking the park for an elegant
lunch or tea.

ÉCOLE DU BREUIL
1867

Address: Bois de Vincennes - Route de la
Ferme - 75012 Paris - tel: 43.28.28.94.
Opening hours: Only the arboretum is
open to the public (daily); entrance fee
on weekends. Telephone for hours.

WHAT TO SEE: The greenhouses; the iris
collection; the landscape garden; the
alpine garden; the rose garden; the
vegetable and fruit garden (open to the
public once a year or to groups by
reservation only); the magnificent
collection of trees in the arboretum: fir,
ginkgo, beech.
INSTRUCTION: Two gardening classes are
offered to the public. Professional
courses include agriculture, gardening,
landscape design, agricultural
technology.

PICPUS CEMETERY
1647

Address: 35, rue de Picpus - 75012 Paris
- tel: 43.44.18.54.
Opening hours: Guided visits are given
April 17 to October 14, 2 p.m. to 6 p.m.;
October 15 to April 16, 2 p.m. to 4 p.m.
Closed Mondays and holidays (entrance
fee).

WHAT TO SEE: This is one of the most
secluded places in Paris: a shady park of
sycamore and ash trees stands in front of
the cemetery, and the white silhouettes
of the nuns from the order of the Sisters
of Perpetual Adoration glide through the
deserted avenues. In the cemetery lie
members of famous French families such
as Chateaubriand, Choiseul, La
Rochefoucauld and Montalembert.

SQUARE DE L'ARSENAL
1983

Address: Boulevard de la Bastille -
75012 Paris.

WHAT TO SEE: This is the harbor for

pleasure boats in Paris. Aside from viewing the boats, you can enjoy the terrace planted with maple trees, a charming arbor covered in climbing roses, and beautiful shrubbery, including privet, blue spiraea, honeysuckle, and knot grass.
ACTIVITIES: Children's play area. This is the departure point for the Saint-Martin canal boat tours.

PARC DE CHOISY
1937

Address: 128-160, avenue de Choisy - 75013 Paris.
Opening hours: Daily 10:30 a.m. to 6 p.m.

WHAT TO SEE: The park has a beautiful collection of trees: Judas, old pear trees, ginkgo bilobas, black pines, paper mulberry; there is an attractive porphyrus table given to France by Finland during the Exhibition of 1937.
ACTIVITIES: Play areas, bowls, swings, puppet theater, snacks, ping-pong.

SQUARE RENÉ-LE-GALL
1938

Address: 43, rue Corvisart - 75013 Paris.

WHAT TO SEE: This is a neoclassical garden from the 1930s with staircases decorated with fossils and pebbles, a neoclassical obelisk surrounded by four arbors covered with climbing roses, and beautiful trees: chestnuts, Japanese sophoras, walnuts, Himalayan pines.
ACTIVITIES: Play area for children, ping-pong, merry-go-round.

PARC KELLERMAN
1939

Address: Boulevard Kellerman or rue de la Poterne-des-Peupliers - 75013 Paris.

ACTIVITIES: Play area for children; football field and tennis courts.

JARDIN DES CINQ-SENS
(GARDEN OF THE FIVE SENSES)
1989

Address: 22, rue Pierre-Gourdault - 75013 Paris - tel: 45.82.05.50.

Opening hours: Monday through Friday 9 a.m. to 3 p.m., for Parisian school children. Visits for small groups can be organized by writing to the museum.

ACTIVITIES: The Maison des Cinq-Sens offers a world of discovery for five- to eight-year-old children. They learn how to develop their five senses in the garden full of flowers, vegetables, fruits, fragrant plants, birds and insects. Specially designed workshops are conducted in the museum. The school is operated by Paris-Espace-Nature.

PARC MONTSOURIS
1878

Address: 2, rue Gazan - 75014 Paris - tel: 45.88.28.60.
Opening hours: 8 a.m. to sunset (in winter); 7 a.m. to 9 p.m. or 10 p.m. (in summer).

WHAT TO SEE: The English-style landscape garden; magnificent trees: copper beech, Chinese pines, tulip trees, black cottonwoods; the lake, home to many different species of duck; the media rose garden: here, every rose was sponsored by a magazine, a newspaper or a television station.
ACTIVITIES: For children: play area, merry-go-round and puppet theater. Summer concerts are given in the bandstand.
RESTAURANTS: Two snack bars sell snacks (weather permitting). *Le Pavillon Montsouris*, 20, rue Gazan (tel: 45.88.38.52); unfortunately, lunch and dinner are no longer served in the garden.

OBSERVATORY GARDEN
1875

Address: 16, boulevard Arago - 75014 Paris.

WHAT TO SEE: This relatively unknown yet beautiful garden is situated in front of the domed Observatory. In front of the main gate, the Paris meridian is symbolized by a metal bar: it is 9 minutes and 21 seconds ahead of Greenwich.

CITÉ UNIVERSITAIRE
1925

Address: 27, boulevard Jourdan - 75014 Paris - tel: 45.89.68.52.
Opening hours: Although the garden is privately owned, it is always open to the public.

WHAT TO SEE: This immense park, which lies in and around dormitory buildings, is planted with rare and beautiful trees. At one time, there were as many as 700 species here, brought back by the creator of the Cité, André Honnorat, from his travels around the world.
ACTIVITIES: The sports facilities (tennis, pool, fields) are reserved for students.

PARC ANDRÉ-CITROËN
The park will be completed in 1993.

Address: 67-69, rue Balard or quai André-Citröen - 75015 Paris - tel: 45.33.51.97.
Opening hours: 7:30 a.m. to 7:30 p.m.

WHAT TO SEE: The white garden, created in 1989, consists of white flowers and minerals; the black garden has black walls and dark-colored plants; there are serial gardens (Metamorphoses garden, Movement garden); a grand canal and many peristyles formed by water; fountains and waterfalls; two monumental greenhouses and six theme greenhouses.
ACTIVITIES: Play area for children.

PARC GEORGES-BRASSENS
1983

Address: Rue des Morillons - 75015 Paris - tel: 45.33.51.97.
Opening hours: 7:30 a.m. to 5 p.m. (in winter), 7:30 a.m. to 10 p.m. (in summer). The park opens at 9 a.m. Saturdays, Sundays and holidays.

WHAT TO SEE: The fragrance garden (eighty varieties of fragrant and aromatic plants), with labels in Braille for sight-impaired visitors; the rose gardens; 1,000 square meters of *pinot noir* vines planted along terraces; a river that falls in a series of cascades; the belfry; the Baltard pavilion; the apiary.
ACTIVITIES: One of the charms of this park is that visitors can stroll and picnic

0   1   2 km

Seine

Square
des Épinettes

Jardin
St-Vincent

Square
des Batignolles

Vignes
de Montmartre

Parc Monceau

Jardins des
Champs-
Élysées

Pala
Roy

Bagatelle

Tuileries

Jardins du
Trocadéro

Jardin
Shakespeare

Lac
Inférieur

École
des Beaux-Arts

Pré Catelan

Jardin
du Ranelagh

Champ
de Mars

2

Bois de Boulogne

1

Jardin
de l'Intendant

Musée
Rodin

3

Malmaison

Lac
Supérieur

Parc des
Missions Étrangère

Allée
aux Cygnes

Unesco

Jardin
de Babylone

Institut
Catholique

Square
Bela Bartok

Luxembourg

Sainte-
Perine

Jardin
des Poètes

École
de Pharmacie

Jar
Ma
Po

Serres
d'Auteuil

Parc
André Citroën

Jardins
Albert Kahn

Parc de St-Cloud

Seine

Parc
Georges Brassens

Villa Adrienne

Villa H

Montsouris

Cité
Universitaire

Vallée aux Loups

Parc de Sceaux

l'Haÿ-
les-Roses

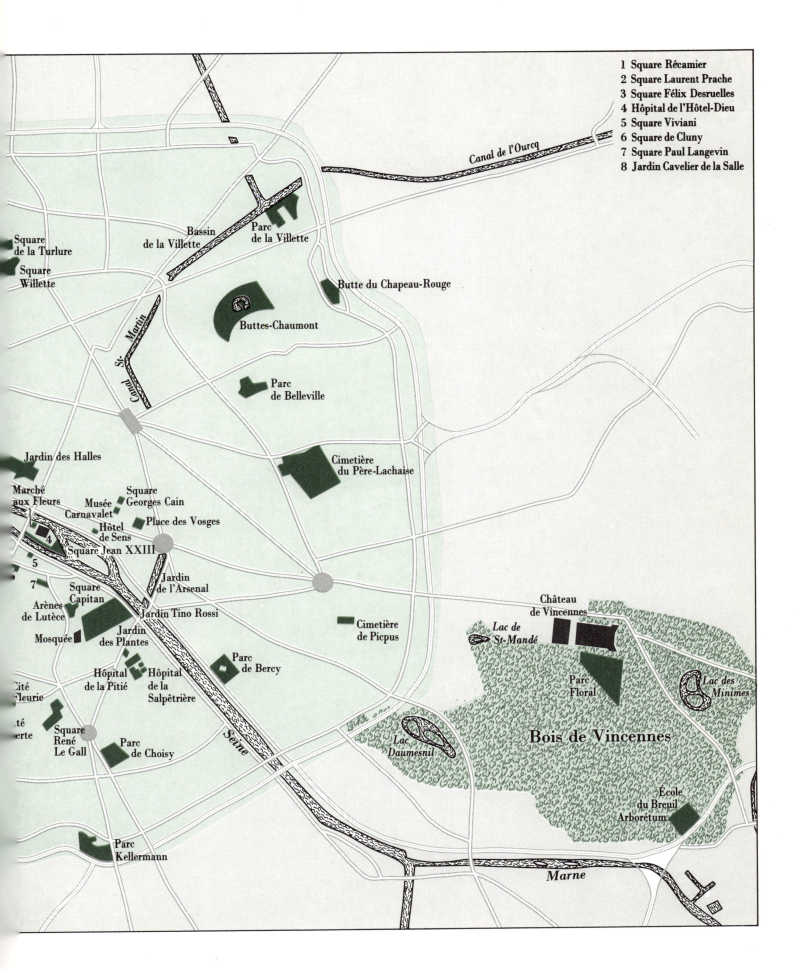

1 Square Récamier
2 Square Laurent Prache
3 Square Félix Desruelles
4 Hôpital de l'Hôtel-Dieu
5 Square Viviani
6 Square de Cluny
7 Square Paul Langevin
8 Jardin Cavelier de la Salle

Canal de l'Ourcq

Bassin
de la Villette

Parc
de la Villette

Square
de la Turlure

Square
Willette

Butte du Chapeau-Rouge

Canal St-Martin

Buttes-Chaumont

Parc
de Belleville

Jardin des Halles

Cimetière
du Père-Lachaise

Marché
aux Fleurs

Musée
Carnavalet

Square
Georges Cain

Place des Vosges

Hôtel
de Sens

4

Square Jean XXIII

5

Jardin
de l'Arsenal

7

Square
Capitan

Jardin Tino Rossi

Arènes
de Lutèce

Mosquée

Jardin
des Plantes

Cimetière
de Picpus

Château
de Vincennes

Lac de
St-Mandé

Cité
Fleurie

Hôpital
de la Pitié

Hôpital
de la
Salpêtrière

Parc de Bercy

Parc
Floral

Lac des
Minimes

té
erte

Square
René
Le Gall

Parc
de Choisy

Seine

Lac
Daumesnil

Bois de Vincennes

Parc
Kellermann

École
du Breuil
Arborétum

Marne

on the grass; there is always a quiet place on the hill to relax and read in the sun. Concerts are given in the bandstand in the summer and an old book market is held every Saturday and Sunday morning. For children: play areas, puppet theater in the summer, grape harvest in the autumn for the children in the nearby schools. A honey festival organized by the Apiculture Association takes place in the autumn (honey is sold in the park).
INSTRUCTION: Bee-keeping classes are given by the Apiculture Association (tel: 45.42.29.08).

SQUARE SAINT-LAMBERT
1933

Address: Rue Théophraste-Renaudot - 75015 Paris.

WHAT TO SEE: This is a typical 1930s garden, consisting of tiers that surround large lawns and an ornamental pond. There are interesting cedrelas and a dozen pterocaryas.
ACTIVITIES: For children: play areas, swings, merry-go-rounds, puppet theater, open-air theater.

ALLÉE DES CYGNES

A walkway bordered with poplars, alders, willows and ash runs the length of this small island in the middle of the Seine. The overrun vegetation is home to many ducks, and in the winter, gulls nest here. Cross to the island from Pont de Grenelle or Pont de Bir-Hakeim.

SQUARE BELA-BARTOK
1981

Address: 55, quai de Grenelle - 75015 Paris.

WHAT TO SEE: A statue of Bela Bartok; a beautiful fountain.

XVIᵉ

BOIS DE BOULOGNE
1852 to 1858

Address: Bois de Boulogne - 75016 Paris.
Opening hours: Jardin d'Acclimatation, 10 a.m. to 6 p.m. (tel: 40.67.90.80).

WHAT TO SEE: Elegant avenues and beautiful walks; two lakes and waterfalls; trees including a pine forest, several oak groves, beech, yoke-elm, birch.
ACTIVITIES: Twenty kilometers of paths and roads (closed to traffic during the weekend); play areas (allée de Longchamp); jogging track (1,600 m); horse-riding center; tennis at the Jean-Bouin stadium; play area at the Relais du Bois, at the intersection of the Croix-Catelan, with a dance hall by the basin. For children, the Jardin d'Acclimatation with its multitude of games and activities is a real treat (entrance fee); a small train runs from Porte Maillot to this area. Rental boats are available on the lower lake (tel: 45.25.44.01); and bicycle rentals. The Museum of Popular Art and Traditions (tel: 40.67.90.00) and a bowling alley (tel: 40.67.94.00) are located on the avenue du Mahatma-Gandhi.
RESTAURANTS: On the lower lake: *Le Chalet des Îles* (tel: 42.88.04.69) is a marvelously pleasant restaurant in the summer, reached by a romantic boat ride. There are many other restaurants, including *L'Orée du Bois* (tel: 42.88.53.87) for lunch, near the children's play area, or *L'Auberge du Bonheur* (tel: 42.24.10.17).

PRÉ CATELAN
1855

SHAKESPEARE GARDEN
1953

Address: Route de la Reine-Marguerite - Bois de Boulogne - 75016 Paris - tel: 45.25.58.05.
Opening hours: 8:30 a.m. or 9 a.m. to 5 p.m., 6 p.m., 7 p.m. or even 8:30 p.m., depending on the season. Closed October 1 to 15. Shakespeare Garden: 3 p.m. to 3:30 p.m. and 4:30 p.m. to 5 p.m. (entrance fee).

WHAT TO SEE: This extraordinary garden has magnificent parterres and remarkable trees: copper beech, sequoia, monkey puzzle tree. The Shakespeare Garden contains all the plants mentioned in the work of the great playwright.
ACTIVITIES: Play area for children; theater performances in the Shakespeare Garden from June to September (tel: 42.76.41.35).
RESTAURANT: *Le Pré Catelan* (tel: 45.24.55.58) is a particularly elegant and luxurious restaurant.

PARC DE BAGATELLE
1905

Address: Route de Sèvres - 92200 Neuilly, or route de la Reine-Marguerite in the Bois de Boulogne - tel: 40.67.97.00.
Opening hours: 8:30 or 9 a.m. to 5 p.m., 6 p.m., 7 p.m. or even 8:30 p.m., depending on the season (entrance fee).

WHAT TO SEE: The English-style and the French-style gardens; the rose gardens; the iris garden; the path lined with wisteria and clematis; the Impressionist garden, complete with pond and water lilies; superb trees: weeping beech, giant sequoia, Corsican black pine, Lebanese cedar. Guided tours of the château are given on Saturdays, Sundays and holidays (tel: 46.51.71.20). The labyrinth is currently under restoration.
ACTIVITIES: The International Competition for New Roses (closed to the public); the Chopin Festival every year in the orangery; concerts and exhibits in the park; visits to the Château de la Muette and the Trianon (tel: 45.01.20.10).
RESTAURANTS: *Les Jardins de Bagatelle*, route de Sèvres (tel: 40.67.98.29). The restaurant and tea room are in the commons constructed by Lord Seymour in the nineteenth century. It is very pleasant to lunch or dine here under the trees, and the restaurant remains open even when the gardens are closed.

AUTEUIL GREENHOUSES
1895 and 1898

Address: 3, avenue de la Porte-d'Auteuil - 75016 Paris - tel: 40.71.75.00.
Opening hours: Daily April 1 to September 30, 10 a.m. to 6 p.m.; October 1 to March 31, 10 a.m. to 5 p.m. (closed if there is snow).

WHAT TO SEE: The remarkable palmarium, with exotic birds at liberty and a pond full of Japanese carp; the tropical greenhouse with exotic plants: banana trees, papyrus. The large greenhouses contain orchids, begonias, ferns. The park has rare and remarkable trees: ginkgo, ailanthus, chestnut trees. There are also masks from Rodin's studio and statues from Versailles.

JARDIN DES POÈTES
1954

Address: Place de la Porte-d'Auteuil -

75016 Paris (entrance on the sidewalk near the interchange of the périphérique).

WHAT TO SEE: This romantic garden, located next to the Auteuil greenhouses and in the middle of a large intersection, is nevertheless an oasis of calm: the lawns are dotted with steles dedicated to French poets: Nerval, Rimbaud, Ronsard, Baudelaire, Verlaine. There is a beautiful statue of Victor Hugo by Rodin.

JARDIN DU RANELAGH
1882

Address: Chaussée de la Muette - 75016 Paris.

WHAT TO SEE: Chestnut, ash and beech trees provide a wonderfully shady area under which children love to play.
ACTIVITIES: For children: play area, swings, bicycle track, puppet theater, a hand-operated antique merry-go-round, a bandstand, a small day-care garden for young children, snack bar.

JARDIN SAINTE-PÉRINE
1977

Address: Avenue de Versailles or rue Mirabeau - 75016 Paris.

WHAT TO SEE: Well hidden and surrounded by houses, this English-style garden has plane, maple, lime and chestnut trees. Beautiful bushes include forsythia, rose, spiraea and currant. There is a beautiful view from the edge of the hollow formed by the garden.
ACTIVITIES: For children: play area, skating track. Dogs are allowed on the path that encircles the park.

TROCADÉRO GARDEN
1879

Address: Place du Trocadéro - 75016 Paris.

WHAT TO SEE: A pleasant garden with rockery and waterfalls; beautiful trees: witch elm, oak. The majestic fountain (twenty jets and fifty-six sprays of water) is turned on at ten minutes to the hour every day (except during freezing weather) from 10 a.m. to 10 p.m.
ACTIVITIES: For children: merry-go-rounds, skating tracks, puppet shows in the summer, snack bars. The Aquarium will reopen in 1993.

RESTAURANT: *Le Totem* (47.27.74.11), with a beautiful terrace, is in the Musée de l'Homme.

SQUARE DES BATIGNOLLES
1862

Address: Place Charles-Fillion - 75017 Paris.

WHAT TO SEE: A picturesque English-style garden; a river and ornamental pool filled with ducks; beautiful trees: plane trees and a Japanese cherry tree that flowers magnificently in the spring.
ACTIVITIES: For children: play area, pedal-cars, snack bars.

SQUARE DES ÉPINETTES
1893

Address: Rue Maria-Deraisme - 75017 Paris.

WHAT TO SEE: A stunning bandstand in the center of the garden; beautiful rows of chestnut trees; trees such as copper beech, silver-leafed lime, soapberry.
ACTIVITIES: For children: play area, swings. For adults: bowls.

SQUARE WILLETTE
1927

Address: Place Saint-Pierre - 75018 Paris.

WHAT TO SEE: A stunning view of Paris from the upper terraces; rare trees at the bottom of the garden: fig, pomegranate, tulip tree, walnut, plane, ginkgo biloba, magnolia.
ACTIVITIES: Play area for children.

VINEYARDS OF MONTMARTRE
1930

Address: Rue des Saules - 75018 Paris.

WHAT TO SEE: This garden, surrounded by small Montmartre houses, was planted with two kinds of grapes: the Gamay and the *pinot noir*. The vineyard

can be visited only through prearranged tours, but it is visible from the street through the fence (for information, call: 40.71.74.00). The Montmartre Museum next door has a delightful small garden planted with fruit trees. It drops from the museum toward the rue Saint-Vincent (open 11 a.m. to 6 p.m.; closed Mondays).
ACTIVITIES: The grapes are harvested in October and a grape-picking festival is held the first Saturday in that month.

SQUARE DE LA TURLURE
1988

Address: Rue de la Bonne - 75018 Paris.

WHAT TO SEE: Arbors covered in wisteria and Virginia creeper; a fountain; old trees such as chestnuts, maples, plane; beautiful view of northern Paris.
ACTIVITIES: Play area for children, bowls.

JARDIN SAINT-VINCENT
1985

Address: Rue Saint-Vincent - 75018 Paris - tel: 43.28.47.63.
Opening hours: From March to the end of October, Saturdays 2 p.m. to 6 p.m. The hours may vary so it is best to call ahead.

WHAT TO SEE: This garden has been left untouched in order to observe which plants and animals live and grow naturally in Paris. There are hedgehogs, aquatic insects, wrens and many kinds of grasses.

SQUARE DE LA BUTTE-DE-CHAPEAU-ROUGE
1938

Address: Boulevard de l'Algérie - 75019 Paris.

WHAT TO SEE: Wide terraces that overlook Pré-Saint-Gervais and the interesting architectural complex of the Robert Debré Hospital; the monumental fountain by Couvègnes; remarkable trees: Kentucky coffee tree, weeping sophora, olive, cedar, apple trees, ginkgo biloba.
ACTIVITIES: Play area for children.

BUTTES-CHAUMONT
1864-1869

Address: Avenue Simon Bolivar or rue de Crimée - 75019 Paris.
Opening hours: 7:30 a.m. to 5:30 to 6 p.m. (in winter), 7:30 a.m. to 9 or 10 p.m. (in summer).

WHAT TO SEE: Magnificent views; the Belvedere; cliffs overlooking the lake; romantic bridges; beautiful trees: evergreen oak, sophoras, Austrian black pines, field maples.
ACTIVITIES: For children: two puppet theaters, pony rides, antique merry-go-round, skating tracks, play areas, swings. There is a bandstand for summer concerts, a boat that crosses the lake, and fishing.
RESTAURANTS: There are three snack bars and three restaurants in the park: *Le Weber* (tel: 42.40.10.47) is an elegant restaurant overlooking the park (open afternoons); *Le Pavillon Puebla* (tel: 42.08.92.62); *Le Pavillon du Lac* (tel: 40.40.00.95), with a terrace at the edge of the lake.

PARC DE LA VILLETTE
1979

Address: 211, avenue Jean-Jaurès - 75019 Paris - tel: 42.40.27.28.

WHAT TO SEE: The follies by Bernard Tschumi; the bamboo garden; Philippe Starck's furnishings; paving by Daniel Buren; the Lion Fountain, the trellis garden.
ACTIVITIES: The children's folly (play area); the video folly; the La Villette house (history of La Villette). There are many activities associated with the buildings on the La Villette site, the largest park in Paris: the Science Museum, the Music School, the Zenith concert hall, the Geode, the Grande Halle.
RESTAURANTS: Several restaurants along the Ourq Canal can be reached by boat, including *Le Croixement* (tel: 42.41.82.00).

ROTONDE DE LA VILLETTE
1935

Address: Place de Stalingrad - 75019 Paris.

WHAT TO SEE: The recently refurbished Ledoux Rotunda. A garden has been created and it is pleasant to sit here and

enjoy the view of La Villette basin and the locks.
ACTIVITIES: Canooing school of the La Villette basin (information available at the Youth and Sports Department of the city of Paris).

— XXᵉ —

PÈRE-LACHAISE CEMETERY
1804

Address: Boulevard de Ménilmontant - rue du Repos - rue des Rondeaux - 75020 Paris - tel: 43.70.70.33.
Opening hours: Daily 7:30, 8, or 8:30 a.m. to 5:30 or 6 p.m., depending on the season and the day of the week.

WHAT TO SEE: Tombs of famous people, including: Molière, Apollinaire, Modigliani, Jim Morrison (guided visits available). This is the largest open green space in Paris, and it features remarkable trees: several species of yew, American walnut, beech.

PARC DE BELLEVILLE
1967-1988

Address: Rue de Couronnes or rue Julien-Lacroix - 75020 Paris - tel: 40.71.74.00.

WHAT TO SEE: The garden, flanking a hill, offers an amazing view of Paris; vast lawns; more than 1,200 trees, including metasequoia, bald cypress, catalpas, soapberry; flower beds filled with perennials; an orangery and a greenhouse; a vineyard (first grape harvest in 1993).
ACTIVITIES: There is a large "Alamo-style" village for children; an amphitheater for free concerts and entertainment. In September 1992 the orangery will become the "House of Air" and will teach schoolchildren all about this subject.

SQUARE SÉVERINE
1933

Address: Boulevard Mortier - 75020 Paris.

WHAT TO SEE: A park with a typical 1930s layout; terraces lined with rows of beautiful trees: Judas trees, ginkgo biloba, tulip trees, honey

locust; dramatic views between the pools.

OUTSKIRTS OF PARIS

ALBERT-KAHN GARDENS
1895 to 1910

Address: 14, rue du Port - 92100 Boulogne-Billancourt - tel: 46.04.52.80.
Opening hours: 11 a.m. to 6 or 7 p.m., depending on the season; closed Mondays (entrance fee).

WHAT TO SEE: This is one of the most interesting parks in the Paris region. Recently restored, this garden-museum includes a beautiful Japanese garden with a spectacular display of azaleas, a French-style garden, an English-style garden, an orchard, a rose garden, a blue forest, a Vosges-style forest and a gold forest, a marsh, and an elegant Second Empire greenhouse.
ACTIVITIES: Permanent exhibition of Albert Kahn's fabulous collection of autochromes; temporary exhibitions on horticulture; a film library with a valuable collection of films made before 1953 (for information about projections call 46.04.52.80); individual consultation of films and autochromes in the exhibition gallery; tea ceremonies in the Japanese garden (Tuesdays and Sundays at 11 a.m.; reservations required); photo, film and sound workshops for eight- to twelve-year-old children; guided visits for groups (reservations required).

PARC DE SAINT-CLOUD
Seventeenth century

Address: Domaine Nationale de Saint-Cloud - 92210 Saint-Cloud tel: 46.02.70.01.
Opening hours: 7 a.m. to 8, 9 or 10 p.m., depending on the season (entrance fee).

WHAT TO SEE: The Cour d'Honneur, the basins, the orangery parterre, the fountain of the Vingt-Quatre Jets, the Trocadéro garden, the French-style gardens, the Rond-Point de la Lanterne, the Grande Cascade, the Breteuil pavilion.
ACTIVITIES: Puppet theater (tel: 60.72.34.23); pony rides (tel: 47.41.86.23); merry-go-round at the Grange aux Écureuils; bicycle and cart rental for children, allée de la Marne (tel: 47.71.64.29); roller skating at the Trocadéro; fun fair in September;

Grandes Eaux (when the fountains are turned on) from May to September on the second and fourth Sundays of the month from 4 to 5 p.m.; Historical Museum (open Saturdays, Sundays, Wednesdays and holidays 2 p.m. to 5 p.m. in winter, 2 p.m. to 6 p.m. in summer).

RESTAURANTS: There are fifteen restaurants in the park, including three that serve light meals: *Chalet de la Manufacture*, *Chalet de l'Allée Verte*, *Chalet de la Félicité*.

The restaurants all have terraces; some offer magnificent views of Paris, others are located in the shade of beautiful trees.

LA MALMAISON

Address: Avenue du Château - 92500 Reuil Malmaison - tel: 47.49.20.07. Opening hours: 10 a.m. to 12:30 p.m. and 1:30 p.m. to 5 p.m. (in winter) or 5:30 p.m. (in summer); closed Tuesdays (entrance fee).

WHAT TO SEE: Romantic garden with a river and small bridges; beautiful trees, including the Marengo cedar; a famous rose garden.

PARC DE SCEAUX
1670

Address: Pavillon de l'Intendance - 92330 Sceaux - tel: 46.61.44.85 and 47.02.52.22 - Museum: 46.61.06.71. Opening hours: 8 a.m. to 5:15 p.m. (in winter), 7 a.m. to 10 p.m. (in summer).

WHAT TO SEE: A magnificent French-style garden with sumptuous views; the Grand Canal, the Aurora pavilion, the stables, the orangery, the waterways. ACTIVITIES: Walks, jogging. The cascades operate every Sunday from the last Sunday in April to the first Sunday in October (also July 14 and August 15).

Guided Tours

• THE CAISSE NATIONALE DES MONUMENTS HISTORIQUES ET DES SITES organizes tours of Buttes-Chaumont, Parc Monceau, Parc Montsouris, Parc de Saint-Cloud, Parc de Sceaux and Parc Georges-Brassens. For information, call: 44.61.20.00.

• THE CITY OF PARIS (Mairie de Paris) organizes guided tours. For information, call: 40.71.75.23.

• THE RUNGIS GREENHOUSES. More than two million plants are grown every year in these greenhouses that cover 109 acres; they are then distributed throughout the Paris parks and gardens. Tours are given in April. For information, call: 46.51.79.92.

• PARIS CÔTÉ JARDIN, 62, rue des Peupliers, 92100 Boulogne. This association offers more than forty guided walks through Paris parks and gardens (June to September). Agronomics specialists lead these initiations into nature within the city. For information, call: 43.10.04.57.

• PARIS ET SON HISTOIRE, 82, rue Taitbout, 75009 Paris. This cultural association organizes tours of the large Paris parks and some of the private gardens. For information, call: 45.26.26.77.

• FONDATION POUR LA CONNAISSANCE DE PARIS ET LE RAYONNEMENT DU TOURISME, 21, rue du Repos, 75020 Paris. This association offers explorations of public and private parks and gardens in Paris organized around four themes: the art of gardening, the art of statuary, literature and ecosystems. For information, call: 43.70.70.87.

LA VALLÉE-AUX-LOUPS
1807 to 1817

Address: Avenue Jean-Jaurès - 92290 Châtenay-Malabry - tel: 46.31.07.02 (for the park) and 47.02.08.62 (for Chateaubriand's house). Opening hours: Daily 9 a.m. to 5:15 p.m. (in winter), 8 a.m. to 10 p.m. (in summer), entrance fee.

WHAT TO SEE: A romantic park with wide oval-shaped lawns; remarkable trees such as the "Josephine" magnolia; an arboretum (currently under restoration); the Valleda tower; Chateaubriand's house (opening hours differ from those of the park; telephone in advance). Nearby is the Parc des Glycines close to the Croux nurseries (1, rue Eugène-Sinet - tel: 46.61.04.06): a landscape park with ginkgo biloba, two 100-year-old beech trees, beds of shrubs and azaleas.

ROSE GARDENS OF L'HAŸ-LES-ROSES
1899

Address: 8, rue Albert-Watel - 94 L'Haÿ-les-Roses - tel: 47.40.04.04. Opening hours: The park is open daily 10 a.m. to 8 p.m. The rose gardens are open only from mid-May to mid-September.

WHAT TO SEE: The rose gardens are in a beautiful park where, even in winter, it is pleasant to stroll. The various rose gardens include the garden for cut flowers, the Madame rose garden, the Malmaison roses, the *gallica* roses, a decorative rose garden, French new roses, foreign roses, a historical rose walk, botanical collections, Asian roses. ACTIVITIES: There are play areas for children throughout the park as well as a picnic area. RESTAURANTS: A snack bar was specially created in the *Pavillon Normand* for hot and cold snacks.

FLORAL CALENDAR

This calendar does not include all the places where you can see these plants and trees; it provides a list of the most spectacular flowering varieties in the parks, gardens and squares of Paris.

CROCUSES *March*
Bagatelle, Luxembourg, Monceau, Montsouris, Buttes-Chaumont, Parc Floral.

TULIPS, DAFFODILS, NARCISSUS *March-April*
Bagatelle, Luxembourg, Monceau, Montsouris, Buttes-Chaumont, Belleville, Georges-Brassens, Malmaison, Pré-Catelan, Parc Floral, Auteil greenhouses, Sceaux, L'Haÿ-les-Roses.

FORSYTHIA *March-April*
Parc Floral, Sainte-Périne, Hôtel de Sully.

MAGNOLIA *March-April*
Bagatelle, Parc Floral, Tino-Rossi, Montsouris, Auteuil greenhouses, Champs-Élysées, Cité des Fleurs, Malmaison.

JUDAS TREE *March*
The spectacular pink flowers bloom in March, before the leaves come out. Jardin des Plantes, Séverine, Willette, Montsouris, Luxembourg.

JASMINE *April-May*
Tino-Rossi, Georges-Brassens, Albert-Kahn, Les Halles.

WISTERIA *April-May*
Parc des Glycines (Croux nurseries), Bagatelle, Georges-Brassens, Square de la Turlure, Les Halles, rue Rembrandt (these wisteria near Parc Monceau are among the most beautiful in Paris).

AZALEAS *April-May*
Bagatelle, Parc Floral, Montsouris, Albert-Kahn, Vallée-aux-Loups.

CAMELIAS *April-May*
Albert-Kahn, Bagatelle, Montsouris, Les Halles, Parc Floral.

PRUNUS *April-May*
The magnificent white and pink spring flowers are found in many gardens, including Luxembourg, Ranelagh, Bagatelle, Parc Floral, Monceau, Montsouris, Jardin des Plantes.

RHODODENDRONS *April-May*
Bagatelle, Parc Floral.

PAULOWNIA *May*
The blue-mauve flowers appear before the leaves. This tree is very well adapted to Paris. There are especially good examples in the Place Furstenberg, Place de l'Estrapade, Place de la Contrescarpe, Marché aux Fleurs, Monceau, Luxembourg.

IRIS *May-June*
Bagatelle, Parc Floral, Jardin des Plantes, Luxembourg.

TULIP TREE *June*
Jardin des Plantes, Monceau, Montsouris, Buttes-Chaumont, Butte-du-Chapeau-Rouge, Willette, Luxembourg, Champ-de-Mars, Épinettes.

CLEMATIS *May to September*
Bagatelle, Buttes-Chaumont, Tino-Rossi.

ROSES *June to September*
Bagatelle, Montsouris, Parc Floral, Parc de Choisy, Jardin des Plantes, Réné-Le Gall, Les Halles, Albert-Kahn, Malmaison, L'Haÿ-les-Roses.

LAVENDER *June to August*
Shakespeare, Kellerman, Tino-Rossi, Georges-Brassens (fragrance garden).

NYMPHEA, LOTUS *July to September*
Bagatelle, Parc Floral, Georges-Brassens, Shakespeare, Auteuil greenhouses.

SOPHORA *Summer*
Bois de Vincennes, Bagatelle, Arènes de Lutèce, Jardin des Plantes, Buttes-Chaumont, Butte-du-Chapeau-Rouge.

MAGNOLIA GRANDIFLORA *July*
Bagatelle, Luxembourg, Auteuil greenhouses.

DAHLIAS *August to October*
Montsouris, Jardin des Plantes, Parc Floral, Bagatelle.

GINKGO BILOBA *Autumn*
The leaves turn a magnificent golden yellow in the autumn. Jardin des Plantes, Vert-Galant, Monceau, Tino-Rossi, Champ-de-Mars, Willette, Buttes-Chaumont, Butte-du-Chapeau-Rouge, Séverine, Père-Lachaise.

VINEYARDS *September-October*
Georges-Brassens, Belleville, Parc Floral, the vineyard at Montmartre, Cité des Fleurs, La Villette, Saint-Vincent.

CHRYSANTHEMUMS *October-November*
Luxembourg (beautiful trailing and flower bed varieties), Auteuil greenhouses, Jardin des Plantes, Monceau, Montsouris, Belleville, Parc Floral.

Throughout the year:

ORCHIDS
Jardin des Plantes, tropical greenhouse at Les Halles, Auteuil greenhouses.

TREE FERNS
Tropical greenhouse at Les Halles.

FICUS, PALM AND BANANA TREES
Auteuil greenhouses, tropical greenhouse at Les Halles, Jardin des Plantes.

BEGONIA, AZALEA, CALADIUM
Auteuil greenhouses.

CAMELIA
Parc Floral.

BAMBOO
Parc Floral, tropical greenhouse at Les Halles, Jardin des Plantes.

CARNIVOROUS PLANTS
Auteuil greenhouses.

BIBLIOGRAPHY

One of the most beautiful books currently available is *Les Promenades de Paris* by Adolphe Alphand, published by Rothschild Éditeurs in 1867-1873. A 1984 reprint, with 560 illustrations (Princeton Architectural Press), is available at the Maison Rustique bookstore, rue Jacob in Paris.

Adams, William Howard. *The French Garden (1500-1800)*. London, 1972.
André, Édouard. *L'Art des jardins*. Paris, 1879; Geneva reprint, 1986.
Arneville, Marie-Blanche d'. *Parcs et Jardins sous le Premier Empire*. Paris, 1981.
Bazin, Germain. *Paradeisos: The Art of the Garden*. New York, 1990.
Benoist-Mechin. *L'Homme et ses jardins*. Paris, 1975.
Berral, Julia S. *Histoire illustrée des jardins*. Paris, 1968.
Blondel, Jean-François. *De la distribution des maisons de plaisance*. 1737; Farnborough reprint, 1967.
Bord, Janet, and Lambert, J.-C. *Labyrinthes et dédales du monde*. Paris, 1977.
Boyceau de la Bareaudière, Jacques. *Traité du jardinage selon les raisons de la nature et de l'art*. Paris, 1638.
Carmontelle. *Jardin de Monceau près de Paris*. Paris, 1779.
Cauquelin, Anne. *L'Invention du paysage*. Paris, 1989.
Caus, Salomon de. *Les Raisons des forces mouvantes avec diverses machines tant utiles que plaisantes*. Frankfurt, 1615.
Chambers, William. *L'Art de distribuer les jardins selon l'usage des Chinois*. Paris, 1761.
Charageat, Marguerite. *L'Art des jardins*. Paris, 1962.
Chevallier, Bernard. *Malmaison, château et domaine des origines à 1904*. Paris, n.d.
Clifford, Derek. *A History of Garden Design*. London, 1962.
Colonna, Francesco. *Hypnertomachia Poliphili*. Venice, 1499; English trans., New York, 1980.

Guides

There are no detailed guides to the many walks that exist in the public parks and gardens of Paris. The most complete information can be obtained in the collection of brochures published by the Park Department of the city of Paris. These "Paris-Nature" brochures are available free of charge at the town hall of each arrondissement. The complete collection of the twenty arrondissements, the Bois de Boulogne and the Bois de Vincennes can be purchased from La Maison de Paris Espace-Nature, Parc Floral, 75012 Paris, tel: 43.28.47.63.

These brochures were a great help to us in writing this book. They list trees, flowers and birds, and include maps that are helpful in finding the most interesting statues and rare trees.

Other less detailed but useful guides include:
Lévêque, Jean-Jacques. *Guide des parcs et jardins de Paris et de la région parisienne*. Paris, n.d.
Racine, Michel. *Le Guide des jardins de France*. Paris, 1990.
Thébaud, Philippe. *Guide des plus beaux jardins d'Île-de-France*. Paris, n.d.
——— *Guide des 300 plus beaux jardins de France*. Paris, n.d.

Conan, Michel. *Preface à trois essais sur le "Beau pittoresque."* Paris, 1982.
Corpechot, Lucien. *Les Jardins de l'intelligence*. Paris, 1912.
——— *Parcs et jardins de France*. Paris, 1937.
Dagognet, Louis, ed. *Mort du paysage. Philosophie et esthétique du paysage*. Paris, 1989.

Deny, Eugène. *Jardins et parcs publics*. Paris, 1893.
Dézallier d'Argenville, Antoine. *Théorie et pratique du Jardinage*. Paris, 1709; reprint of the edition completed in 1747, Geneva, 1984.
Duchêne, Achille. *Jardins de l'avenir*. Paris, 1931.
Forestier, Jean-Claude Nicolas. *Grandes villes et systèmes de parcs*. Paris, 1906.
Ganay, Ernest de. *Beaux jardins de France*. Paris, 1950.
——— *André Le Nôtre*. Paris, 1962.
Girardin, René-Louis de. *De la composition des paysages*. Paris, 1777; reprint (with a postscript by Michel Conan), Paris, 1979.
Grimal, Pierre. *L'Art des jardins*. Paris, 1974.
Gromort, Georges. *L'Art des jardins*. Paris; reprint 1988.
Hautecœur, Louis. *Les Jardins des dieux et des hommes*. Paris, 1959.
Hazelhurst, Franklin-Hamilton. *Jacques Boyceau and the French Formal Garden*. Nashville, 1966.
——— *Gardens of Illusion. The Genius of André Le Nôtre*. Nashville, 1980.
Hegel, Georg Wilhelm Friedrich. *Aesthetics*. Vol. 1, part 1. New York, 1983.
Jeannel, Bernard. *Le Nôtre*. Paris, 1985.
Johnson, Hugh. *Principles of Gardening*. London, 1979.
King, Ronald. *The Quest for Paradise*. Leicester, 1979.
Kretzulesco-Quaranta, Emanuela. *Les Jardins du songe*. Paris, 1976.
Lassus, Bernard. *Une poétique du paysage: le démesurable*. Paris, 1976.
Le Corbusier. *La Charte d'Athènes*. Paris, 1943.
Luginbuhl, Yves. *Paysages*. Paris, 1989.
Mallet, Robert. *Jardins et paradis*. Paris, 1959.
Marrey, Bernard. *La Grande histoire des serres et jardins d'hiver*. Paris, 1983.
Mollet, André. *Le Jardin de plaisir*. Stockholm, 1851; Paris reprint, 1981.
Mollet, Claude. *Théâtre des plans et jardinages*. Paris, 1652.

Morel, Jean-Marie. *Théorie des jardins.* Paris, 1776.

Plumptre, George. *Garden Ornament: Five Hundred Years of History and Practice.* London, 1989.

Thacker, Christopher. *The History of Gardens.* San Francisco, 1979.

Thouin, Gustave. *Plans raisonnés de toutes les espèces de jardins.* Paris, 1821; Paris reprint, 1988.

Vacherot, Jules. *Les Parcs et jardins au commencement du XXe siècle.* Paris, 1908.

Véra, André. *Le Nouveau jardin.* Paris, 1913.

Watelet, Claude-Henri. *Essai sur les jardins.* Paris, 1764.

Wiebenson, Dora. *The Picturesque Garden in France.* Princeton, 1978.

Woodbridge, Kenneth. *Princely Gardens: The Origins and Development of the French Formal Style.* New York, 1986.

Catalogues and periodicals

"Architecture et paysage." *Technique et Architecture* 370, Paris, February-March 1987.

Le Concours de la Villette. Catalogue of the exhibition at Centre Pompidou, Paris, 1980.

Jardins botaniques et arboretums de France. Paris, 1975.

Les Fleurs dans les jardins au XVIIe siècle. Catalogue of the exhibition held for the centenary of the horticultural ENS, Versailles, 1974.

Grandes et petites heures du parc Monceau. Catalogue of the exhibition at the Cernuschi Museum, Paris, 1981.

"Inventaire des parcs et jardins de la région parisienne: les 4 premiers secteurs visités." Paris, 1985.

"Les Jardins." *Monuments Historiques* 5, 1976.

"Jardins contre nature." *Traverses,* October 1976.

Jardins de Paris. Catalogue of the exhibition at the Town Hall of the 13th arrondissement. Paris, 1984.

"Jardins parisiens et Jardins des provinces." *Monuments Historiques* 142 and 143, January and March 1986.

Jardins en France (1760-1820). Catalogue of the Caisse Nationale des

Monuments Historiques et des Sites exhibition. Paris, 1978.

Les Arbres remarquables des promenades et jardins de Paris. Paris, 1983.

"Parc-Ville Villette." *Vaisseau de Pierres* 2, 1987.

Parcs et promenades de Paris. Catalogue of the exhibition at the Pavillon de l'Arsenal. Paris, 1989.

Paris 1937. Catalogue of the 50th anniversary exhibition. Paris, 1987.

"Paris, le retour de la ville." *Architecture-intérieure-Crée* 192-3, 1983.

"Paysages: parcs urbains et suburbains." *Cahiers du CCI* 4 (1988).

The Picturesque Garden and its Influence outside the British Isles. minutes of the symposium, Washington, 1974.

Works about Paris gardens

Apollinaire, Guillaume. *Le Flâneur des deux rives.* Paris, 1918.

Aragon, Louis. *Le Paysan de Paris.* Paris, 1926.

Barthélémy, Guy. *Les Jardiniers du Roy: petit histoire du Jardin des plantes de Paris.* Paris, 1979.

Baudelaire, Charles. *The Painter of Modern Life and Other Essays.* New York, 1986.

Benjamin, Walter. *Paris, capitale du XIXe siècle.* Paris, 1989.

Bergeron, Louis, ed. *Paris, genèse d'un paysage.* Paris, 1989.

Boubat, Edouard and Noël, Bernard. *Jardins et squares.* Paris, 1982.

Buyer, Xavier de. *Fontaines de Paris.* Paris, 1987.

Champigneulle, Bernard. *Promenades dans les jardins de Paris, ses bois, ses squares.* Paris, 1965.

——— *Paris, architecture, sites et jardins.* Paris, 1973.

Chateaubriand, René de. *Mémoires d'outre-tombe.* Paris.

Daguesseau, André. *Les Jardins de Paris, poésies descriptives.* Paris, 1956.

Dupays, Paul. *Paris agreste.* Paris, 1952.

Fargue, Léon-Paul. *Le Piéton de Paris.* Paris, 1939.

Folain, Jean. *Paris.* Paris, 1978.

France, Anatole. *Le Livre de mon ami.* Paris, 1885; reprint, 1985.

Giraudoux, Jean. *Pleins Pouvoirs.* Paris, 1948.

Haussmann, Baron. *Mémoires.* Paris, 1890-1893; reprint, 1979.

Heron de Villefosse, René. *Prés et bois parisiens.* Paris, 1942.

Hillairet, Jacques. *Le Palais royal et impérial des Tuileries et son jardin.* Paris, 1965.

——— *Dictionnaire historique des rues de Paris.* Paris, 1975.

Hugo, Victor. *Les Misérables* and *Notre-Dame de Paris.* Paris, 1962.

Joannis, Claudette. *Les Petits métiers des jardins publics.* Le Puy, 1977.

Lavedan, Pierre. *Histoire de l'urbanisme à Paris.* Paris, 1975.

Leroy, André. *Bagatelle et ses jardins.* Paris, 1956.

Loyer, François. *Paris: Nineteenth Century.* New York, 1989.

Marin, Louis. "L'Art des jardins et les mouvements de l'esprit humain; le Luxembourg, jardin classique et paysager" (manuscript). Paris, 1970.

Perret, Jacques. *Le Jardin des Plantes.* Paris, 1984.

Pilon, E. *Le Jardin des Plantes.* Paris, 1926.

Poète, Marcel. *La promenade à Paris.* Paris, 1913.

Une Vie de cité, Paris. Paris, 1925.

Poisson, Georges. *Guide des statues de Paris.* Paris, 1990.

Queffelec, Henri. *Jardins de Paris.* Rennes, 1990.

Reda, Jacques. *Les Ruines de Paris.* Paris, 1985.

——— *Châteaux des courants d'air.* Paris, 1987.

Richard, Patrice. *Jardins secrets de Paris.* Paris, 1980.

Selvaggi, ed. *Le Jardin du Luxembourg.* Paris, 1980.

Soprani, Anne. *Paris-Jardins.* Paris, 1986.

Thezy, Marie de. *Paris, la rue: le mobilier urbain parisien du Second empire à nos jours.* Paris, 1976.

Vallée, Claude. *Places et jardins de Paris.* Paris, 1962.

Vezin, Luc. *Les Artistes du jardin des Plantes.* Paris, 1990.

Zola, Emile. *Les Rougon-Macquart.* Paris, 1969-1970.

INDEX

ACKNOWLEDGEMENTS

The authors extend their warmest thanks to all the people and organizations who were kind enough to help and advise them during the preparation of this book, particularly André-Georges Haudricourt, Tangi Le Dantec, Alain Melizi and Chauval Potart.

Denise Le Dantec and Jean-Pierre Le Dantec would also like to express their gratitude to Madeleine Deschamps for her encouragement during the writing of this book.

The publisher would like to thank those people who allowed the gardens to be photographed and who provided the essential information for the garden guide, particularly: Yves Bouedec, Jean-Noël Burte, Maris-José Gambard, Marie-Françoise Hamard, Daniel Laurentiaux and Jean-Luc Sizorn.

Appreciation is also extended to Jean-Loup Arenou, Gérard Bagenge, Jeanne Beausoleil, M. Belamine, Joseph Belmont, Jérémie Benoît, Marie-Françoise Boutin, Nelly Chamaux, Roger Claudel, Gilles Clément, Dominique Coutart, Éric Defretin, M. Dulocty, M. Houssin, Françoise Jacquier, D. Maurel, M. Michelangeli, Guy Nicot, M. Ondella, Michel Pichon, Alain Plagnes, Father Michel Quesnel, M. Regnier, M. Richard, Alain Richert, M. Roy, Yolande Thiriet, Bernard Viel, Jacques Vilain, Alain Woisson.

And finally, many thanks to Raphaël Sorin and Gérard-Julien Salvy for their advice and assistance.